Coasters of the 1970s (Volume 2)

by

Bernard McCall

It seems astonishing that ocean-going ships were built at Korneuburg near Vienna in Austria. DDSG (The Donaudampfschiffahrtsgesellschaft - Danube Steamboat Shipping Company), established in 1829 and then the world's largest shipping company, used Korneuburg for wintering and also repairing its vessels. Its growth into a shipbuilding yard is detailed on page 37. The *Rinkö* was a sistership of *Gimo Celtica* on that page. The early years of both ships are complex because of ownership transfers. Suffice it to say here that in January 1973 both came into the ownership of Peter Döhle. She had been launched on 8 April 1972 and was completed as *Hainburg* on 24 June. In Döhle ownership, she was renamed *Nad Monarch* and in late 1974 became *Atlantic Earl*. In June 1997 she was bought by Norwegian owners. Renamed *Ringve*, in 1998 her tweendeck was removed and she was converted to a self-discharger. She joined the Paal Wilson fleet in 1990 and was renamed *Rinkö*. Laid up in Stavanger between July 2000 and October 2002, she was then bought by Greek owners and renamed *Rinko I*. She became *Unity* in 2003, *Kevser II* in 2006 and was recycled at Aliaga in June 2011.

(John Mattison)

INTRODUCTION

In Volume 1, we looked at ships that had been built in shipyards in the UK, Ireland and the Netherlands. In this volume, we look at ships built elsewhere in the world. We begin in Germany, then move to Scandinavia, southern and central Europe, and finally Japan. As far as shipbuilding was concerned, this decade really was one of globalisation.

As I wrote in the introduction to the previous volume, the 1970s was a decade of rapid and astonishing change in shipping. Coal was declining as a domestic fuel but the most dramatic change was the growth of containerisation as a means of transporting goods. At the start of the decade, ships with masts and derricks were commonplace but by the end of the 1970s, there was an ever-growing demand for container feeder ships which had no gear but relied on shore-based infrastructure.

Also in the first volume, we referred to the development of sea/river ships. We can look at these ships in much more detail in this volume as many of them were built at yards in Germany although it must be said that yards in other countries also produced coasters designed for both inland and seagoing navigation. In this context, it is important that we give some consideration to the huge number of ships built to trade on the inland waterways of Russia.

In the captions, we have tried to say something about the yards which built the ships. The inclusion of such information in Volume 1 attracted much favourable comment and we are pleased to continue with similar notes herein. The 1970s began with great optimism but this faded away during the decade and it is sad to see how many shipyards disappeared during that time. Others saw mergers and takeovers and were able to survive longer but the number of European yards still building ships in the 21st century is a tiny fraction of those that were busy in 1970.

Acknowledgements

Once again it is simply impossible to name the many people who have helped with this book. Some have answered a solitary question; others have provided a huge amount of information. I hope that all will accept these general words of thanks. I must, though, acknowledge the constant help and support of Gil Mayes and Bent Mikkelsen. I readily thank the staff of Amadeus Press for their work. It would be equally difficult to acknowledge all the books to which I have referred. The publications of the World Ship Society and of Gert Uwe Detlefsen have been invaluable.

Bernard McCall   Portishead   September 2016

Published by Bernard McCall, 400 Nore Road, Portishead, Bristol, BS20 8EZ, England.
Website : www.coastalshipping.co.uk.   Telephone/fax : 01275 846178.   Email : bernard@coastalshipping.co.uk.
All distribution enquiries should be addressed to the publisher.
Printed by The Amadeus Press, Ezra House, 26 West Business Park, Cleckheaton, BD19 4TQ.
Telephone : 01274 863210.   Fax: 01274 863211.   Email: info@amadeuspress.co.uk;   Website : www.amadeuspress.co.uk.
ISBN : 978-1-902953-79-3

Front cover : The rain clouds are not too far away as the **Maria Graebe** was photographed in the River Ouse. She was one of a class of ten vessels built for Günther Graebe at the Hugo Peters shipyard in Wewelsfleth. They were arguably the most stylish coastal container ships ever built. Like several others in the class, her hull was subcontracted to Stader Werft (see page 24). She was launched as **Maria Graebe** on 22 June 1971 but delivered as **Kungsbron** on 25 September. She reverted to **Maria Graebe** in 1973. With Reederei Günther Graebe in financial difficulties in early 1983, she was sold within Germany and renamed **Euro Freighter**. Later sales and renamings saw her become **Janica** (1987), **Lona** and then **Luna** (1988), **Mika** (1992), **Star II** (2003) and finally **Sue** (2007). She grounded off Nisyros Island on 13 December 2007. Although refloated on 15 January 2008, repairs were thought to be uneconomical. She was laid up and eventually recycled at Aliaga in December 2012.

(David Gallichan)

Back cover : In 1962, Per Henriksen signed a contract to buy a new ship simply to reduce his tax bill. His Mercandia group later became one of the largest shipping companies in Denmark. The **Mercandian Sky** was subcontracted from Büsumer Werft to the Heinrich Brand yard in Oldenburg where she was launched on 11 March 1975 with completion on 15 April. Sold in June 1981, she was renamed **Pep Antares**. Later in her career she was renamed **Pav Trader** (1984), **Per Trader** and **Petra II** (1986), **Artax** (1988), **Tramarco Sailor** (1989), **Sailor** (1993) and **Progress Lily** (1994). She was recycled at Alang in February 2011. The Heinrich Brand shipyard was established in 1850 by Heinrich Christian Brand. In 1917 the yard moved to a bigger site and then started to build steel ships. It remained in family ownership until hit by bankruptcy in 1995. An immediate attempt to continue shipbuilding saw the formation of Neue (New) Brand Werft but this too was forced to close in 1997.

(David Gallichan)

We begin with ships built by some of Germany's inland shipyards. Ruhrorter Schiffswerft was established in Duisburg-Ruhrort on the River Rhine in 1921 and taken over by Krupp in 1938, then being known as Friedrich Krupp Ruhrorter Schiffswerft. Its most successful period was between the 1960s and 1970s. It was taken over in 1993 and has since been known as Neue Ruhrorter Schiffswerft. Having been a prolific builder of inland craft, it was hardly surprising that it should try construction of the new generation of sea/river vessels being designed and built in the late 1970s. Two coasters were built during the 1970s, both with fixed bridge, followed by a further five in the mid-1980s. The second of the two in the 1970s was the **Ute-V**, launched on 13 May 1978 and delivered on 30 June. We see her passing Meredyke inward bound on the River Trent. She was sold and renamed **Kirsten** in 1989 and four years later was converted to a suction dredger named **Pays De Loire** for work in western France. In 2013 she was sold and renamed **Durrat al Manama**.

(David Gallichan)

The company known as Kölner Werft was founded in Duisburg on 1 December 1866 by Ewald Berninghaus. Initially boilermakers, the company moved into shipbuilding in 1873. After the death of the founder, his son Caspar took over and soon became a leading authority on inland shipbuilding. In 1929 the company took over a shipyard at Köln (Cologne) and began to build sea/river ships including two passenger ships with Voith-Schneider propulsion for work on the River Rhine. The construction of two ammonia tankers in the mid-1950s resulted in the yard specialising in chemical tankers. From 1965, shipbuilding was concentrated on the Köln yard. Lack of demand for inland vessels in the mid-1970s led to bankruptcy and the final ship was completed at the Gutehoffnungshütte shipyard in Walsum. This was the **Capella**, a newsprint carrier with ramp on the port side and two pallet elevators. Launched on 9 September 1976, she was delivered to Duisburg-based Rohden Shipping on 22 December. She was sold and renamed **Bremer Norden** in 1990 and became **Hanseatic Sea** in 2004. We see her at Port-St-Louis-du-Rhône in southern France on 11 October 2008. She was recycled at Aliaga during February 2012.

(*Annemarie van Oers*)

One of the most astonishing shipbuilding stories is that of the Arminius shipyard at Bodenwerder which is on the River Weser and about 165 miles (260km) from the open sea. The yard had traditionally built inland waterway vessels but in the mid-1970s, the hulls of three coasters were subcontracted to the yard by the Cassens shipyard in Emden. The **Herm Kiepe** was one of the three. She was launched on 17 May 1975 and seven days later two tugs took the hull down the tortuous River Weser to Emden for fitting out. She was delivered to her owner on 10 July. Sold within Germany and renamed **Hera** in August 1986, she survived until May 2012 when she was delivered to Grenå in Denmark for recycling. We see her in the locks at Holtenau, near Kiel, prior to heading west along the Kiel Canal on 7 November 1998 on a voyage from Falkenberg to Bremerhaven. The shipyard continues to be busy building and repairing inland waterway vessels.

(Neil Burns)

Until the early 20th century, Wörth was the focal point of the industry on the River Main. With the noise of the shipyards there giving rise to constant complaints and also prompted by the need to build larger vessels, Anton Schellenberger moved his construction yard across the Main to Erlenbach in 1917 and established Bayerische Schiffbau GmbH in the following year. The yard built military vessels during World War 2 and after Erlenbach had been taken over by American forces in 1945 the yard was used to repair bridges over the Main. Taken into Austrian ownership in 1996, the yard continues to build and repair mainly inland vessels. The **Estestrom** was delivered as **Bianca** in June 1970 to Hamburg-based A Kirsten & Co KG. She was the second of a pair of ships to be used on her owner's liner service from Rhine and Main ports to the Iberian peninsula. Intended to trade mainly from Frankfurt, they could reach that port only rarely because of the river height. They were ahead of their time - the Rhine and Main were not yet ready for container transport. She became **Estestrom** in 1975 following a sale to Julius Hauschildt, also of Hamburg. She reverted to **Bianca** after purchase by Mediterranean owners in 1987. Later changes of name saw her become **Sea Bianca** (1989), **Alsena** (1994), **Christina K** (1999) and **Gerasimos** (2008). Some sources suggest she was renamed **NS Hunter** in 2007 but this is not correct. She has not traded since 2012 and she is thought to be laid up at Astakos in western Greece. She is seen outward bound in the River Ouse on 14 April 1981.

(David Gallichan)

After a gap of several years, the Bayerische yard returned to shipbuilding in the late 1970s and in September 1978 the *Merlan* was launched. The coaster was delivered to Captain Ulf Ahrens on 28 November as **Sea Merlan**, the name change resulting from a 19-year time charter to Freight Express Seacon Ltd. The charter was not renewed. In 1980 her owner Captain Ahrens had sadly died on board when poisoned by noxious gases during an inspection of the cargo. His good friend Captain Frank Dahl took over ownership and at Delfzijl on 23 December 1997 he renamed the ship **Denika** after his sons Dennis and Annika. In 2004 the ship was sold within Germany and was renamed **Jutland**. Although sold to Greek owners and renamed **Ios Island** in 2013, she was sold for recycling at Aliaga in June 2014. She is seen on 25 February at Dunball Wharf on the River Parrett as she discharged granite setts from Leixoes.

(Author's collection)

On the eastern side of the River Usk at Newport is Orb Jetty, also known as Lysaght's Wharf. Both names are appropriate as John Lysaght built Orb steelworks and the jetty was initially used to discharge steel brought from the owner's works by the River Trent. Now deemed unsafe for use, it was used latterly mainly for the export of steel products from Llanwern. The **Brigitta** was photographed at the jetty on 28 September 2003. Having built one of the initial 'Cargo Liner' series in 1973 (see page 17), the Kötter Werft shipyard at Haren on the River Ems built a further three sea/river coasters in 1977. She was launched on 17 October 1979, being completed as **Emstal** on 8 December.

She was renamed **Ostergotland** briefly in 1980 but had reverted to her original name by 1981. She became **Brigitta** in 1989 and finally **A.P. Smile** in 2004. By 2011 her continued existence was in doubt and she was deleted from registers. The Kötter Werft yard was established in 1919 by ships' carpenter Rudolf Kötter. The first new steel ship was an inland bunker tanker built in 1958 and the first coaster was built in 1966. The yard remains open in the ownership of the Kötter family and concentrates on the construction and repair of inland waterway vessels.

(Cedric Catt)

Another of the coasters from Kötter Werft was the appropriately-named **Ems-Liner**, launched on 18 December 1976 and completed in March 1977. Having passed through the ownership of various companies, she was bought by Faversham Ships in late 1998 and became **Conformity** on 17 November. After six years excellent service, she was sold to Russian owners and renamed **Fairwind** under the flag of Dominica. Her name was amended to **Fairwind I** and she switched to the Panamanian flag in 2008. A sale in March 2010 saw her become **San Marini** and she was recycled at Aliaga in August 2011. We see the **Conformity** in the River Usk on 25 August 2002 at the end of a voyage from Aviles. She was approaching Birdport which was originally the Channel Drydock of the Union Dry Dock company. This was taken over by Bell Lines in 1964 and used as a container terminal and became Birdport in 1994 after Bell Lines transferred its sevices to Avonmouth. It handles a wide variety of cargoes in addition to the steel formerly shipped via Orb Jetty.

(Bernard McCall)

The shipyard of Jos L Meyer at Papenburg on the River Ems has become synonymous with the construction of large cruise vessels. Some forty years ago, however, the yard was building a much wider variety of vessels including coasters. The *Ina* was launched at the yard on 2 December 1978 and delivered as *Germann* to Unitas Schiffahrts in Haren/Ems on 30 December. In 1986, she moved to Dutch ownership with Wagenborg as manager and was renamed *Algerak*. She remained in Wagenborg management after a sale within the Netherlands in mid-1990, being renamed *Auriga* at Delfzijl on 30 June. In December 2000 she was renamed *Ina* after sale to Baltramp Shipping, of Szczecin. She retained this name following sale to Turkish owners in 2010 but three years later a sale within Turkey saw her become *Kumsal D* under the flag of the Cook Islands, switching to that of Moldova in late 2013. She was photographed at Coleraine as she loaded scrap for Bilbao on 14 May 2003.

(Stan Tedford)

We do not usually include roll on / roll off vessels in our surveys but such ships were becoming increasingly significant during the 1970s and should to be represented. We have selected an interesting example. The **Black Sea Star** was one of five sister vessels and was the second of two built at the Hermann Sürken shipyard in Papenburg; the other three were built in Turkey. She was launched as **Thiassi** but completed as **Irish Trader** on 10 February 1972. She was chartered by Monarch Lines Ltd for a service from New Ross to France but this did not work out and she soon reverted to **Thiassi**. In 1974 she was sold and renamed **Viirelaid**, joining her four sisterships in Russian ownership. The next sale saw her become **Black Sea Star** after a sale in 1997. She was detained at Immingham in late August 2001, the inspection being abandoned after 26 deficiencies were found. She was given permission to sail to Alblasserdam, near Rotterdam, arriving there in March 2002 and photographed as dawn broke on a July morning.

(Dominic McCall)

The deficiencies noted in that report were eventually rectified and in early 2003 the **Black Sea Star** was sold to owners based in Sharjah and was renamed **Berbera Star**, departing for the Middle East in late January. She was photographed at Sharjah on 2 February 2004. We understand that she has now been broken up but we have no details. The Hermann Sürken shipyard opened in 1946. During the 1980s, the yard built a large number of low air draught coasters but it suffered bankruptcy in mid-1992. Unlike some other yards that feature in this book, no rescue package could be organised to save the Sürken shipyard.

(Roger Hurcombe)

This vessel was launched at the Martin Jansen shipyard in Leer on 5 December 1975 and on 3 February 1976 was completed as **Cairncarrier** for Shaw, Savill & Albion. She was the fourth of five sisterships which occupied the yard's production in the mid-1970s. Her first sale came in 1982 when she was renamed **Tequila Sunset** and six years later she became **Arklow Bridge** following sale to an Irish company in which Arklow Shipping had a 50% share. After only two years she was sold and renamed **Wave Rose**. The next two years saw a series of name changes, these being **Armour** (1993), **Eurolink** (1997), **Varun** and then **Mirage** (2004), **Nejib M** (2005) and finally **Meryam S** (2010). In 2016 she remains in service for Syrian owners. In our photograph, she is about to pass Ellesmere Port when outward bound on the Manchester Ship Canal. The Jansen shipyard was opened in 1927 and remained family-owned until closure through bankruptcy in 1987. The yard was subsequently re-opened for shipbuilding by Dutch builder Ferus Smit.

(David Gallichan)

The **Alexander** was the last of four almost identical vessels built at the Jansen yard. We see her passing beneath the Humber Bridge in 1984. She was launched on 24 March 1979 and completed for Hubert Kiepe of Haren/Ems on 6 June. After arriving at Rotterdam from Bilbao on 3 October 1994, she was laid up and was sold at auction on 14 December. The buyer was Danish owner Carsten Rousing and the ship, renamed **Sarah Rousing** after the owner's daughter, left the Dutch port on 31 December bound for Søby where she was rebuilt with a much heavier tank top to allow her to carry scrap and heavy steel products. She traded to the steel works at Frederiksværk delivering cargoes of scrap and loading finished steel and later for H J Hansen, a company also involved in the handling of scrap. A restructuring of the Rousing company resulted in the **Sarah Rousing** being transferred to RMS and she was renamed **RMS Copenhagen** in September 2010. Within a year, however, she was sold for recycling, the work being carried out at Odense by, ironically, H J Hansen.

(David Gallichan)

From Leer we move to Emden at the mouth of the River Ems and this marks the end of our look at coasters built in upriver shipyards. In 1883 Johann Hermann Schulte and Christoph Bruns opened a shipbroking company at Papenburg. Ten years later Johann Schulte opened an office in Emden as he realised the the opening of the Ems-Dortmund Canal (in 1897) would enhance trading possibilities. In 1918 Schulte & Bruns opened a shipyard in Emden, initially to repair the company's barges. The company was declared bankrupt in October 1977 although offshoots started by family members survived and part of the site was taken over by Cassens Werft in 1979. Obviously many of the company's ships were built at its own yard. The **Katrin Schulte**, launched there on 7 March 1972 and completed on 26 April, was one of several small ships built for the Baltic trade in the early 1970s. Sold to Swiss owners in 1983, she was renamed **Murten** and later became **Roermond** (1994), **Murten** again (1995) and finally **Virgo** (also 1995). She was deleted from registers in 2011 as her continued existence was in doubt. She is seen passing beneath the Severn Bridge on 9 July 1979.

(Cedric Catt)

The other major shipyard in Emden was that of Cassens. It was here that the **Rhône-Liner** was launched on 21 April 1978 and completed on 30 June. She was built for the Gerhard Wessels fleet and immediately went on charter to RMS. In late 1981 she was bareboat chartered by Jugobrod-Beoplov and spent some time trading in the Black Sea as **Smederovo** before returning to northern Europe and her original name a year later. In 1989 she was transferred to Duisburg-based See-transit, a company specialising in the transport of steel. She was fitted with a new engine and renamed **Rhine-Liner**.

We see her as such arriving at Orb Jetty from Duisburg on 16 May 2004. Later in the year she was sold and renamed **Orfeus**. Shipbuilding in Emden can be traced back to the 15th century and the history of Cassens goes back to 1672. The construction of steel ships began in 1902 when Cassens moved to its present site. The company, part of the Werftunion Group, faced insolvency twice in the first decade of the present century but has managed to survive by skilful restructuring.

(Dominic McCall)

14

On 14 September 1979, the *Heljo* was delivered from Cassens Werft to Heinrich Kiepe, of Haren/Ems. At that date, the yard was trading under the name of Werftunion. She started life on charter to Duisburg-based Rhein Nord Ostsee Befrachtungsgesellschaft mbH (RNO) which specialised in bringing timber from the Baltic to Rhine ports and returning with finished steel. In 1989 she was bought by Norwegian owners and renamed *Norbox*. On 25 June 1995 she was purchased by Danish captain/owner Carsten Rousing and the ship was taken over at Bergen on 9 August. Named *Anders Rousing,* she immediately sailed to Søby Motorfabrik & Stålskibsværft to be rebuilt in the same way as *Sarah Rousing* (page 12). She was delivered to Grenå for recycling on 28 December 2011. We see her inward bound in the Odense canal with a cargo of sand on 18 May 2009.

(Bent Mikkelsen)

The first of a pair of sisterships, this coaster was launched at the Jadewerft shipyard in Wilhelmshaven on 1 April 1978 and delivered to Shamrock Shipping as **David Dorman** in June. Three years later the company and both ships were sold to James Fisher plc, of Barrow. In 1984 she was bareboat chartered by Glasgow-based J & A Gardner with Dennison Shipping taking over as bareboat charterer in 1988 and renaming her **Deer Sound** in the following year. She was repossessed by James Fisher after the collapse of Dennison Shipping in 1994 and laid up at Birkenhead. She was soon sold to Alderney Shipping and, now named **Isis**, placed on that company's Channel Islands services with a weekly voyage to Rotterdam where she used the Ridderhaven container terminal. We see her at St Peter Port, Guernsey, in July 2002. In summer 2011 she was sold, along with her sistership, to the Great Glen Shipping Company for trading in north-west Scotland. Both have been hugely successful carrying mainly timber but also bulk cargoes such as aggregates and salt. The Jadewerft yard opened on 2 June 1948, initially repairing vessels damaged during World War 2. Following bankruptcy in 1979, it was revived as Neue (New) Jadewerft. In 2004, it became part of the Bremen-based Lürssen Group and now specialises in repairing and refitting luxury mega yachts in addition to work on military vessels.

(Dominic McCall)

The Wessels family, based in Haren-Ems, has always been forward thinking and in the mid-1970s Captain Gerhard Wessels gave new impetus to a long-standing concept. Coasters fitted or adapted for upriver trading had long been in existence but Captain Wessels and his team, drawing heavily on the designs of inland pusher tugs and container-carrying barges, produced a vessel with a lifting wheelhouse, a long single hold, and measurements that made them narrow in comparison to their length. The latter feature made them suitable for canal locks. Six vessels of the 'Cargo-Liner' design were ordered, four coming from the Schlömer shipyard at Oldersum on the River Ems, a yard that had built mainly barges and fishing vessels. The **Cargo-Liner V** was launched on 24 April 1975 and delivered on 23 May. Sold in 1981, she was renamed **Inez V** and became **Argo** in 1983, and **Compaen** in 1993. She was laid up at Leer on 15 October 1997 and was eventually sold in July 1999. Her new owner took her back to the Schlömer shipyard where she was converted into a barge and renamed **Cornelis**. She became **Tuimelaar** in June 2000. All six ships were modified, notably being fitted with a much larger bridge. This view shows **Argo** passing Aggersund on 26 March 1993. The Schlömer shipyard is still in existence. Now called the Diedrich shipyard, its main work is ship repair.

(Bent Mikkelsen)

Launched at the Elsflether Werft shipyard in Elsfleth on 5 December 1979, this vessel only just made it into the book as she was completed on 29 December. Initially named **Canopus**, this was modified to **Canopus I** on 22 August 1994. At the time, she was on charter to Geest North Sea Line for its container service linking Rotterdam to Hull and Ipswich, and she remained on that service. In 2000 she was renamed **Nadine** and became **Opus** two years later. She was photographed on 15 July 2008 as she approached Goole with a cargo of wind turbine towers. In 2012 she was acquired by Romanian owners and renamed **Sibel J** and in 2016 she was still trading mainly in the Black Sea. Elsflether Werft was established in 1916 and soon expanded to build vessels of all kinds. In the Second World War the yard specialised in the conversion of fishing vessels to patrol boats for the Kriegsmarine. With orders hard to obtain during the 1970s, the yard began to build luxury yachts and sailing ships. The owning company was restructured in 1996. It immediately ceased all newbuilding and has since concentrated on repairs and modifications.

(Simon Smith)

Conrad Lühring took over a shipyard in Brake in 1870. Initially building wooden sailing vessels, Conrad's sons Hinrich and Friedrich introduced iron vessels and steam power in the early 20th century. Bankruptcy caused closure of the yard in 1988, by which time it had built some 350 vessels. On 28 April 1979 the coaster **Antares** was delivered from the yard to Captain Gerhard Litmeyer, of Haren/Ems, and she entered service for RMS. She was the second of three almost identical sisterships. In mid-June 1997 she was sold to Norwegian operator Flekkefjord Shipping and renamed **Anette**. She was photographed on 1 November 2003 as she approached the dock at Tilbury with a cargo of packaged timber. In the early hours of 29 June 2010 she collided with the Danish coaster **Livarden** near Haugesund. She was on passage from Aalborg to Poti and had a pilot on board. She suffered damage to her starboard side and berthed at Kopervik. In May 2012 she was sold to Irish operator Coast Lines Shipping Ltd and was refurbished at the former Verolme Cork shipyard in the Republic of Ireland. She re-entered service as **Ayress** under the flag of Dominica and since that time has traded successfully in the round timber trade from western Scotland.

(Dominic McCall)

On 29 January 1971, the **Island Commodore** was launched at the Rolandwerft shipyard in Berne, near Bremen, for Portsmouth-based Commodore Transporters Ltd and she was delivered two months later. Lengthened by 10 metres in 1977, she was intended for the Portsmouth - Channel Islands service and she remained on this service following sale in 1990 to Huelin-Renouf, a company based in the islands since the early 1930s. She was renamed **Huelin Dispatch** and kept this name until late April 1996 when a newer vessel took over the service and the name. Now named simply **Dispatch**, she moved to Southampton awaiting sale.

(Author's collection)

In mid-October 1996 the **Dispatch** was acquired by Portuguese owners and her name was shortened once again when she became **Patch**. She arrived at Viana do Costelo on 25 June 1999 and was later arrested. She was sold to owners in the Middle East in 2003 and resumed service as **Nader II**. She became **Bassma** in 2007 and **Lady Dina** in 2010. We see her at Alexandria on 13 April 2011. She was recycled at Aliaga in October 2012.

(Tony Hogwood)

The Rolandwerft shipyard opened in 1913 for the construction of boats and yachts but soon began to build warships. By 1963, 262 seagoing ships had been built but only nine years later, the company was bankrupt. On 1 July 1972, Rolandwerft was taken over by Detlef Hegemann and initially undertook only repairs and the construction of ship sections. It was in 1977 that building started on the first ship and this was the **Verena**, photographed when about to pass beneath the Humber Bridge on 9 August 1983. She was launched on 18 February 1978 and completed on 24 May. In 1992 she joined the fledgling fleet of Dundalk Shipping and was renamed **Rockisland**. After the demise of this company she was laid up at Manchester from 28 June 1998 until sold to Greek owners in July 1999, being renamed **Lady Georgia**. Sold and renamed **Chrissoula S** in 2008, she was recycled at Aliaga in 2015. In April 2010, the Lürssen Group acquired Detlef Hegemann Rolandwerft.

(David Gallichan)

Our journey through Germany now takes us to the major shipyards on or near the River Elbe. The River Stör is the Elbe's longest tributary and flows into the Elbe just beyond the town of Wewelsfleth, the location of the Hugo Peters shipyard. The **Christopher Meeder** was launched at this yard on 31 March 1976 and completed on 13 May. An ideal container feeder, she spent much of the 1990s trading between Liverpool and Belfast with occasional calls at Cardiff, Greenock and Dublin. We see her inward bound to Cardiff from Belfast on 23 August 1997. In late 2002 she was sold to Danish company Dannebrog

and renamed **Kronborg** under the British flag. By June 2003 she was trading between Tarragona and Salerno but a year later she was serving Gdansk and Gdynia from Rotterdam and Bremerhaven. She remained under the British flag after being sold and renamed **Sea Pearl** in mid-March 2005. After just over a year, she was sold and renamed **Sparrow** under the flag of Sierra Leone. She left Antwerp as such on 6 June 2006 and headed initially for Casablanca prior to trading in the Mediterranean and Black Sea. She is still trading in that same area.

(Nigel Jones)

Offering a very different profile from the Hugo Peters yard was the *Aqua Star*, photographed at Gdynia on 28 July 2002. She was launched on 9 June 1979 and delivered as **Susanne L** to Captain Gerhard Lange on 30 June. She retained the characteristic integrated funnel and bridge that had become a feature of the Peters yard but was fitted with two 3.5 tonne derricks. In 1984 she was chartered by Bremen-based Bruno Bischoff and renamed **Bremer Mercur**. She reverted to her original name in 1985 but in 1989 the Bischoff charter was renewed, this time for six years. It was on 1 September 1995 that she became **Susanne L** once again. The sequence was broken in 1999 when she was sold and renamed **Aqua Star**. She became **Susann** in 2004. On 8 January 2006 she capsized and sank 80 miles off Sfax when on passage to this port from Castellon. Her crew of six was rescued. Despite suffering various crises in recent years, the Peters shipyard still survives. It was founded by Jürgen Peters in 1871 and has concentrated on the building of mega yachts since 2004 although cargo ships have not been ignored.

(Dominic McCall)

Shipbuilding started in Stade, on the western side of the River Elbe, in the 17th century but the name Stader Schiffswerft was not used until 1927. Between 1937 and the yard's closure in 1967, 53 coasters were built. In 1969, the yard re-opened under new ownership and began to build hulls subcontracted from other yards that were extremely busy. The Hugo Peters yard subcontracted the hull construction of several vessels to Stader Schiffswerft. One of these was **Kiefernberg**, launched on 6 February 1970 and completed on 4 April.

She was the third vessel in a series for Lübeck-based Günther Graebe and these vessels were the first full container ships designed at the Peters yard. Sold in 1987, she was renamed **Gardwind**, becoming **Wardwind** and **Grenland** in 2002. She was wrecked at the entrance to the Spanish port of Avilés on 21 February 2006. We see her in the River Ouse on 3 June 1978 when on charter to Iggesund, a Swedish company manufacturing paper products.

(Laurie Schofield)

The Scheel & Jöhnk shipyard in the Harburg area of Hamburg was opened in March 1933 on the site of the Schloß yard of Reinhold F Holtz (founder of Norderwerft - see pages 28/29) which had been forced to close through lack of orders during the Great Depression. The yard continues to exist for repairs and newbuildings although now named Jöhnkwerft following a takeover in 2006. To all intents and purposes, the *Ara* seems to be identical to the class of sleek vessels built at the Hugo Peters shipyard but she is one of a pair built by Scheel & Jöhnk. When launched, she was named **Schwarzenberg** and thus appeared to follow the naming pattern of the Günther Graebe ships. Her

owner, however, was a Walter Jöhnk. We must assume that Herr Jöhnk wanted his two new ships built at his own yard and purchased the design from the Hugo Peters yard. Completed in mid-December 1970, she had several names during her career, these being **Sara** (1985), **Ara** (1986), **Janor** (1993), **Ara** (1995), **Ami** (2001), **Hazem** (2002), **Naera** (2003), **Lady Maha** (2004) and finally **Constantza** (2005). She was recycled at Aliaga in March 2011. We see her approaching Goole with timber from Varberg and illuminated by a rare shaft of sunlight on 2 March 1997.

(John Mattison)

There can be no doubt that the most prolific coaster building yard in western Europe during the 1970s was that of J J Sietas located at Neuenfelde on the outskirts of Hamburg. The yard's history goes back to 1635 but it came into the ownership of Johann Jakob Sietas in 1895. From the 1950s, it established a hugely successful system of building to standard designs with its designers always seeming able to anticipate the needs of shipowners. In 1968 construction began of the Type 58 design, nominally a containership with an 87TEU capacity. This design was also suited to general cargo and especially the carriage of timber. The last two in the series were chartered from new to Aros Line which delivered timber from Scandinavia to the UK. The **Arosette** was the last of the type to be built. She was launched on 20 November 1971 and delivered on 16 December to, appropriately, Johann Jakob Sietas Reederei. In January 2002 she arrived at Bremerhaven with major engine damage. She was sold to Syrian owners and fitted with a new engine, eventually leaving Germany as **Khadijeh** in the autumn. On 11 January 2003, she suffered a further engine problem when off Lesbos. Her cargo of timber shifted and she sank two days later after the crew had abandonded ship.

(David Gallichan)

For a second vessel from the Sietas yard, we have selected an example of the popular Type 104 low air draught design. The first of the eleven constructed was the **Condor** which was one of six coasters built for Paul Häse and fitted with tanks for the carriage of china clay slurry from Par and Fowey. She was launched on 21 November 1978 and delivered on 20 December. She traded successfully for twenty years, often taking slurry to inland ports on the River Rhine or River Seine and returning to the UK with steel. Sold to Dutch owners in mid-1998, she was renamed **Bernice** and arrived at Scheveningen to have six tanks fitted in her hold for the carriage of vegetable oil. We see her at Kaliningrad on 2 November 2004 following arrival from Szczecin. She was sold to Bulgarian owners and renamed **Nani** in 2008 and arrived at Aliaga for recycling in September 2010. The Sietas yard was an unexpected victim of the worldwide recession in 2009 and by 2014 had merged with the Pella shipyard in St Petersburg to form Pella Sietas.

(Ron Wood)

Such was the demand for ships from the J J Sietas shipyard in the early 1970s that some vessels had to be subcontracted to the Norderwerft shipyard in Hamburg. The Type 81 design was a feeder container ship of which twenty-two examples were built in the mid-1970s. The ships had a capacity of 144TEU and were hugely popular with charterers. This vessel was launched at the Norderwerft shipyard as **Komet** on 15 August 1975 and she was delivered as **Saracen Prince** on 16 September and became **Komet I** in 1976. Two years later she was renamed **Bourgogne** by her charterers and retained this name until October 1989 when she became **Heinrich Behrmann** following sale to Heino Behrmann. In March 2004 she was shuttling between Hamburg and Bremerhaven but was sold and renamed **Karina Kokoeva** at the end of the month becoming **Karina K** in January 2005. Exactly two years later, she left Bergen at the start of a voyage to the Black Sea and was sold for trading as **Lady Amneh** under the flag of Georgia. In 2010 she was sold and renamed **Steamer** and as such was recycled at Aliaga in mid-August 2014. The Norderwerft yard was taken over by the Lürssen Group in 2012. We see her as **Bourgogne** at Eastham on 26 May 1978.

(Laurie Schofield)

Another of the Type 81 container feeders was the **Nautilus**, the tenth of the twenty-two ships of this design. She was launched as **Nautilus** on 25 April 1975 and delivered on 25 June as **American Cherokee**, one of four examples of the type that were chartered by United States Lines and named after native American tribes. Owned by Hans Herman Knüppel, of Hamburg, she reverted to **Nautilus** on completion of the charter in 1979. She was renamed **Coburg** following a sale within Germany in 1988. In March 1996 she was sold to Hydrogas, a divison of chemical giant Norsk Hydro, and from late May until June she was converted to a tanker for the carriage of liquid carbon dioxide and was renamed **Hydrogas III**. Yara demerged from Norsk Hydro in 2004 and the tanker was renamed **Yara Gas III**. In June 2016, Yara sold its European liquid cardon dioxide interests to Praxair, an American company. The three tankers were included in the sale and this vessel was renamed **Iduna**. We see her as **Hydrogas III** at the dedicated import terminal at Purfleet on the River Thames on 10 October 2004. The houses to the left are on a road known as Harrisons Wharf.

(Bernard McCall)

The 1970s saw the development of bridge-forward designs, an interesting example being this vessel built as **Areucon Caroline** for Arabian-European Lines but soon renamed **Helena Husmann**. In 1982 she was lengthened by 20 metres. She was renamed **Conro Trader** in 1985 and her design proved ideal for the rapidly-expanding trade in the carriage of windfarm equipment. In 2010 she was sold to owners in Ukraine and was rebuilt and converted to a rail ferry at the Kherson shipyard. She then entered service carrying railway tank wagons across the strait between Kerch and Kavkaz. She was reported to be operated by TPP-Terminal, one of the largest and oldest oil traders in Crimea, and was being used to deliver supplies to that area currently occupied and annexed by Russia. The story of her construction is complex. D W Kremer

Sohn had a shipyard at Elmshorn on the narrow River Krückau. In 1971 the company opened a second yard at Glückstadt offering more space. In May 1975, the company suffered serious financial problems and in July it was sold to Harms Bergung, a Hamburg ship owner. From mid-1976 only the yard at Glückstadt was used and the company was finally bankrupt in April 1978. At the time, the **Areucon Caroline** was one of four vessels being built. Her hull had been constructed at the HDW yard in Kiel and she was being fitted out at Glückstadt. She was thus the last ship to be contracted to Kremer Werft although all sources suggest that she was built by HDW.

(Koos Goudriaan)

There are two major shipyards at Rendsburg on the Kiel Canal. The Nobiskrug yard opened in 1905 and was on the verge of bankruptcy in 1986 but was saved when taken over by HDW, of Kiel. The yard now builds mega yachts. The **Detlef Schmidt** was launched at the Nobiskrug yard on 14 September 1978 and delivered to owner Johannes Ick on 31 October. Lengthened by 16,8 metres in August 1994, this increased her container capacity from 142TEU to 231TEU. She remained in Ick ownership although renamed **Marianne** in 1994. For much of her career she was on charter to Team Lines for its feeder services from Hamburg and Bremerhaven to Scandinavia and we see her outward bound in the River Elbe in February 1994. In early summer 2001, with a sale imminent, she served Antwerp and Rotterdam from Hamburg. After completion of the sale, she left Hamburg on 12 July 2001 with Jeddah as her destination. She was renamed **Al-Gaga** and, under the flag of Saudi Arabia, began to trade between Jeddah, Port Sudan and Hodeidah. Later changes of name saw her become **Jamal** and then **Mariam** in 2010 and **Diamond** in 2011. In 2016 she continues to trade in the Middle East.

(Bernard McCall)

The other shipyard at Rendsburg is Krögerwerft. The brothers Hans Kröger and Karl Kröger along with naval architect Walter Brauer established a shipyard at Warnemünde, near Rostock, in 1928. In 1945 the yard was taken over by Russia and Warnowwerft was established on the site. Three years later the brothers established a shipyard at Schacht-Audorf on the southern bank of the Kiel Canal at Rendsburg. It was taken over by the Lürssen group in 1987. The yard has concentrated on the construction of mega yachts since 2003 but has also undertaken ship repairs. Although a prolific builder of ships in the 1970s, the number of dry cargo coasters built and completed at the yard was small. One of the few was the *Ulsnis*, launched on 24 May 1978 and completed on 10 July. Sold and renamed *Urania* in 1989, she became *Eide Junior* in 2000 after sale to Norwegian owners by whom she was converted to a self-discharger with the fitting of a Kobelco SK330LC grab. Sales within Norway saw her renamed *Fjordtor I* in 2010 and *Bulk Trans* in 2014. We see her at Odense on 6 August 2002, three days after her arrival from the Norwegian port of Harstad.

(Oliver Sesemann)

The story of the Kröger brothers is rather more complex because they also acquired the shipyard at Husum in north-west Germany. This vessel was launched at the Schacht-Audorf yard on 22 April 1977 but completed at Husum as **Theodor Storm** on 29 June. In 1978 she was taken on charter but despite being renamed **Baltic Heron**, she traded to Bilbao from ports such as Ellesmere Port, Portsmouth and Warrenpoint. We see her approaching Eastham on 9 February 1980. Reverting to **Theodor Storm** in 1983, she then traded in the eastern Mediterranean until late summer 1985 when the next charter saw her renamed **Somers Isles** for trade between Jacksonville (later

Fernandina Beach) and Hamilton, Bermuda. In autumn 1999 she returned to Europe as **Theodor Storm** but for several weeks official movement reports confused her with her replacement that had been renamed **Somers Isles** so exact details are unclear. In early January 2000 she was sold to Erwin Strahlmann and, now named **Sprinter**, was working in the general cargo trades. Sold to Russian owners in Vladivostock in 2005 she was renamed **Fortuna** and in 2016 continues to trade in eastern Russia, China and South Korea.

(David Gallichan)

Emphasising the link between the Husumer shipyard and the Kröger brothers, this vessel was launched at Husum as **Hans Kröger** on 6 July 1973 and completed on 8 September for Reinhard Danz. She immediately went on charter for two years as **Baltic Consort**, and she reverted to this name for a shorter charter in 1977. Having become **Hans Kröger** once again in 1978, she then spent some time on charter to Swedish company Aros Line without change of name. In June 1989 she was chartered by Dragon Line and renamed **Brynmore**, trading mainly from Swansea and Garston to Antwerp and Rotterdam. In December 1990, Bruno Bischoff took over the charter at St Petersburg and she became **Bremer Wappen** and initially traded between that port and Rostock. She was still in Danz ownership when renamed **Kilia** in

1992 but after trading between northern Europe and Casablanca she was bought by Moroccan owners in 1993 and renamed **Oued Ziz**, becoming **Kalila** in 1994 when she worked on a liner service linking Rotterdam, London and Rouen to Casablanca. We see her at Rotterdam on 5 October 1995. In 1999 she was sold and renamed **Bam Sea** and in 2008 Turkish owners gave her the name **Murvet Imamoglu**. She was recycled at Aliaga in April 2013. Shipbuilding in Husum can be dated as far back as 1606 but the Kröger brothers opened their yard in January 1947. The site of the yard moved to Husum's outer harbour in the early 1970s. Declared bankrupt in 1999, the company was taken over for the manufacture of wind turbines although part of the site is still used for ship repair.

(Bernard McCall)

The **Bushra 1** was the first of four sisterships built for Iraqi Marine Transport (Iraqi Line), of Baghdad, by Büsumer Werft. She was launched on 21 May 1976 and delivered to her owners as **Aledreesi** on 30 July. She arrived at Basra from Singapore Roads on 22 September 1980 and remained blocked there until September 1988. By the time of her first sale, in 2002, she had disappeared from movement reports. She was renamed **Hashin** and became **Bushra I** in the following year. We see her at Sharjah on 21 February 2003. By this time she had been considerably modified. Her masts and four 5-tonne cranes had been removed and replaced by a small deck crane. Her hull had been fitted with sponsons. She was renamed **Suad N** in 2005 and became **Nazim N** under the flag of Georgia in 2006. Her final name, bestowed in 2007, was **Almarwa** and she was recycled as such at Aliaga in August 2011. The shipyard at Büsum in north-west Germany opened in 1901. During the 1970s it specialised in the construction of chemical tankers and refrigerated vessels. The yard closed on 30 September 1986.

(Roger Hurcombe)

A boatyard had been established at Boizenburg on the River Elbe in 1793 and the yard's first steel ship was launched in 1895. Located in the German Democratic Republic (GDR) following the division of the country, the Elbewerft yard soon concentrated on the production of vessels for eastern Europe. In 1970/71, it built 14 handy-sized cargo ships of 299grt for the state-owned merchant fleet of the GDR with a further 2 for Russia. The ships built in 1971 were given names of German towns ending in ___ow and were fitted with two 3-tonne cranes. The **Satow** was launched on 2 March 1971 and completed on 25 November. Sold to Greek owners in 1991, she was renamed **Porfirios**.

She later became **Mermaid II** and **Good Hope II** in 1999 and then **Hadil** and **Golden I** in 2002. She is understood to be still in service in the Middle East. That series of 14 was immediately followed by 5 longer ships of a similar design (plus 2 for Russia) but intended for the carriage of containers. One of these was **Kropelin** which was launched on 9 June 1972 and completed on 27 September. Acquired by Belgian owners in 1992, she was converted to an edible oil tanker and remains in service as **Star Aruba**. The **Satow** and **Kropelin** are seen at Par on 12 December 1988.

(Cedric Catt)

The first slipway at Korneuberg in Austria was erected in 1864. Between 1938 and 1945 the shipyard was incorporated into the Hermann Göring Works and was declared to be of strategic military importance, and expanded to this end. As well as the considerable expansion of the shipbuilding facilities personnel was also increased to around 1,300 employees. Following the occupation of Korneuburg in 1945 the shipyard was placed under Soviet administration, operations were continued, and ships were produced for Russia. In 1955 the shipyard was returned to the DDSG. Over the years it built passenger ships, floating cranes, tugs, barges, trawlers - and some ocean-going ships. Much of the yard's output was bought by communist countries and the collapse of these in the early 1990s led to the closure of the yard in November 1993. The site was acquired by the municipality of Korneuburg and, now called Blue Danube Park, is used for offices and recreation. It is the venue of an annual harbour festival. Appropriately this vessel was launched as **Korneuburg** on 23 December 1971 and completed on 22 June 1972. She had fourteen names during her career, too many to list here, but was called **Gimo Celtica** between mid-February and mid-October 1990. She is seen at Watchet on 7 September 1990. Remarkably the last twelve years of her career were the most settled. In 2002 she was bought by Norwegian owner Rolf Wagle and was converted to a selfdischarging bulk carrier with the fitting of an Åkerman 620 excavator. Named **Linda** she ultimately arrived at Grenå for recycling in July 2014.

(Bernard McCall)

Elite Shipping was established in 1976 as a brokering company handling mainly cargoes of timber being shipped from the Baltic to the eastern Mediterranean. This proved to be very successful and a newbuilding was ordered from the Nordsøværftet shipyard in Ringkøbing. This yard built a further thirty ships for Elite Shipping over the next thirteen years. The company also quickly invested in secondhand tonnage and became commercial managers and part owners of two coasters built by Nordsøværftet. The second of these was **Roselil** which was launched on 30 August 1978 and delivered on 3 November. Following takeover by Elite Shipping in July 1983,

she was renamed **Arktis Rose** and four months later was lengthened by twelve metres by Fredericia Skibsværft. We see her approaching the Humber Bridge on 27 April 1984. She was renamed **Arktis Orion** in 1987. The year 1994 saw a hire purchase deal with a Chinese buyer but this collapsed and she was sold and renamed **Transource 1** in 1997. A sale in 1999 saw her become **Blue Orion** and the final sale was to a Libyan owner in 2007. She eventually stranded near Ras al Hial on the Libyan coast after being gutted by fire.

(Bernard McCall)

The Nordsøværftet shipyard at Ringkøbing opened on 1 August 1958 and closed in September 1997. Much of the output of the yard in the 1970s comprised 61 examples of a standard class but at the end of the decade two low air draught vessels were built for the London & Rochester Trading Company. The second of these was **Quiescence** which was launched on 13 September 1979 and delivered on 26 October. We see her undergoing trials in lively conditions on Ringkøbing Fjord prior to delivery. The Danish flag can be seen through the spray at the stern of the ship. She was laid up at Otterham Quay on 4 April 1997 and departed on 11 April 1998 as **Euro Bulk** after sale to Norwegian owners. A sale within Norway in 1998 saw her become **Sveabulk**. Once in Norwegian ownership, she was fitted with a Komatsu excavator and grab. She continues to trade along the Norwegian coast.

(Nordsøværftet archive, courtesy Bent Mikkelsen)

The **Piquence** was the sistership of **Quiescence** and was launched on 8 June 1979 with delivery being effected on 7 September. Both vessels were built to trade along the River Rhône and were followed in this area by other vessels in the fleet of their owners. On cessation of this trade, **Piquence** was laid up at Otterham Quay three days after her sister in 1997 and one year later she was sold to Norwegian owners and renamed **Euro Trans**. She left the Kent port on 20 October for Swijnouscie where she was fitted out as a self-discharger with the addition of a Kobelco excavator and grab. We see her arriving at the Danish port of Horsens on 8 August 2004. Although still flying the Norwegian flag, she was owned by JK Shipping in Denmark between 2004 and 2010. It is unlikely that she will trade again as she has been awaiting repairs at Klaipeda for over two years.

(Bent Mikkelsen)

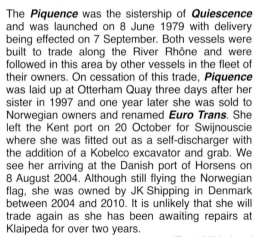

The 1970s saw a huge output from two shipyards in Frederikshavn. The older of the two was Frederikshavn Værft & Flydedok, funded by DFDS and established in 1913 on the ruins of H J Buhls Skibsværft which opened in 1871. The first ship was delivered in 1915. The yard saw constant expansion over the next fifty years. The yard was sold in 1981 and taken over by J Lauritzen Holding, the parent company of DFDS. Henceforth it was known as Danyard. Closure came in 1989. The yard built 79 ships for the Mercandia Group over a period of 21 years including a group of nine in the early 1970s, one of which was **Merc Aequator**. This vessel was launched on 22 January 1973 and completed on 9 March for Per Henriksen's Mercandia company. She was the fourth of the nine sisterships. In October 1979 she was sold to owners in Jakarta and was renamed **Niaga XXII** and a further sale within Indonesia saw her become **Rachmanuel II** in 1988. We see her thus named when anchored in Singapore Roads on 17 June 1999. She was sold for recycling at Chittagong in May 2006.

(Nigel Jones)

Frederikshavn Værft also built a large number of gearless coasters. One of these was the **Skanlith**, launched on 11 December 1973 and completed on 15 March 1974. In 1983 she was sold to Swedish owners and her name changed to **Skanlill**. Her next change of identity came in 1999 and again it required but few strokes of a paint brush when she became **Skantic**. Our photograph show her about to pass beneath the Humber Bridge on 5 April 2007. She was sold following bankruptcy in 2012 to buyers in West Africa after being laid up in Svendborg since October 2009. Renamed **El Elohim**, she was fitted with a modern crane amidships and, now registered in Togo, passed through the English Channel on 21 September 2012. She continues to trade along the African coast and seems to work out of Lome in Equatorial Guinea.

(Simon Smith)

The other major shipyard in Frederikshavn is Ørskov Christensens Stålskibsværft which was opened in October 1958. Initially fishing vessels were built but once Copenhagen-based shipowner Otto Danielsen became involved with the company, the construction of coasters began in 1962. After the closure of Danyard, the company took over some of that yard's facilities, notably its drydocks. Early in the present millennium, the company had to be restructured but it remains in the ownership of the Ørskov Christensen family. The **Alice Bewa**, the prototype of a series of fourteen sisterships, was launched at the yard on 28 May 1971 and delivered on 15 October. When built, she had a third tripod mast with two derricks amidships which she retained after being sold and renamed **Horsa** in 1976. By the time she had become **Gibhawk** in 1983, the midships mast had been removed. We see her outward bound from Ayr on 11 April 1983. By the end of that year, she had been renamed **Collette**. Later changes of name saw her become **Montechristo** (1984), **Sabrina** and **Ageliki K** (1987), **Agel** (1989) and **Union Star 62** (2002). Now owned in Indonesia, she continues to trade in the Far East.

(Bernard McCall)

Danish owner Ejnar Nygaard bought his first ship in 1931. In 1943 he established the Danena shipping company, the letters "Dan" coming from Danmark and "ena" coming from Ejnar Nygaard and his home city of Aarhus. As his fleet had grown in size over the previous fifteen years, he wanted his own shipyard and the port of Aalborg offered him space in the Skudehavnen. There he built a yard named Limfjords-Værftet which was opened in 1947. From 1984 until its closure in 2003, the yard only repaired ships. The **Dania**, launched on 18 September 1970 and delivered to Danena on 16 July 1971, was the only coaster built at the yard during the 1970s. We see her at Aberdeen on 31 August 2005. The ship was initially contracted for carrying steel products, especially rods and plates, from the steel works at Oxelösund in Sweden mainly to the UK. From the late 1970s, however, **Dania** was laid up at Limfjords-Værftet because Ejnar Nygaard refused to sail when there were no profits. The ship was sold in late 1987. She was detained and laid up at Rudkøbing on 21 January 2009 following a port state control inspection, moving to Marstal for contuing lay up on 18 June. In September 2010 she was sold to Gabon-based owners and renamed **Dania Express** but never sailed as such. In April 2012, she was renamed **Rosalina II** and arrived at Dakar on 14 June. She is reported to have been renamed **Tatiana Estrella** in 2014.

(Alastair Paterson)

The **Esther Bech** was one of a group of seven vessels built at the Sønderborg shipyard in southern Denmark. The lines of these vessels were decidedly unattractive but they were designed for a very specific purpose. The design featured a large cargo space in the aft section where cable drums could be stored when the vessels were used in seismic survey work. Owners Bech-Rederierne worked in partnership with the American company Western Geophysical. The **Esther Bech** was the last of the five sisterships delivered to the Bech company, the last two being contracted by Bech but taken over by

Mohrship, of Svendborg. She was launched on 21 February 1975 and delivered on 31 May. In December 1977 she was taken over by Mohrship and was renamed **Esther Silvana** in June 1978, becoming **Birdie** following a sale within Denmark in December 1980. This was brief as she was sold to Caribbean operators in mid-January 1981 and renamed **Carib Dawn**. On 4 January 2001 she arrived at Tuxpan from Belize City for breaking up. She was photographed as she approached Eastham on 29 October 1977.

(David Gallichan)

The shipyard at Bogense was always overshadowed by the much larger yard at nearby Lindø. The Bogense yard was opened in 1925 and closed in 1989. There was an attempt to revive it with the rebuild of a trawler and construction of two offshore supply ships but bankruptcy was declared in February 1992. Some of the facilities are used for boat repair. The **Hanne Mette** was one of five distinctive sisterships. Completed for Danish owners as **Horneland** in April 1978, she was sold and renamed **Hanne Mette** in 1987. We see her on 19 September 1998 outward bound from Marchwood military port to Bourgas. In May 2003 she was laid up at Svendborg after owner/captain Knud Olsen decided to retire. He remained on board, however, so that he could use the

owning company's resources without paying tax as masters on board ships do not pay tax according to Danish law. In March 2004 she was sold to Hanne Hansen, of Svendborg, and sailed to that port to continue lay up. Although officially renamed **Hanne Hansen**, this name was never painted on the ship. She left northern Europe in late summer 2004 after being sold to owners based in Panama and was renamed **Deborah I** for trade around the Cape Verde Islands. Little more is known about her although a photograph of her at Dakar, Senegal, in 2009 shows her with a cargo of containers and with all gear removed.

(Chris Bancroft)

The **Aasfjord** has been owned by companies in several different Scandinavian countries. She was launched by Svendborg Skibsværft on 12 May 1978 and delivered to Danish owners Mortensen & Lange as **Charm** in July 1978. In May 1982 she was bought by owners in Iceland and renamed **Keflavik**. The new owners had paid a hefty price for the ship because her Danish operators had been trading her very profitably in the paper trade from Canada to the USA and Caribbean. Sold within Iceland in 1989, she became **Irafoss** and then in 1997 she entered Norwegian ownership following purchase by Aasen Shipping. She was renamed **Aasfjord** and was rebuilt as a self-discharger fitted with a Hitachi EX600 excavator and grab. In September 2011 she was sold to owners based in Las Palmas and transferred to the flag of Panama as **Altair**. In 2015 she traded to Las Palmas from ports such as Lisbon, Casablanca and Cartagena. Wooden ships were built at the Svendborg yard from 1867 and the first steel ship was built in 1907. It remained prosperous until 1992. Despite the best intentions and plans of several owners, the yard eventually closed in 2001. We see **Aasfjord** outward bound in the River Thames on 17 July 1999.

(Ian Willett)

We have just one coaster built at a yard in Sweden. The **Alice** was launched at the yard of Falkenbergs Varv on 7 September 1973 and delivered to Swedish owners in January of the following year. In early 1993 she was sold and renamed **Afrodite** under the flag of St Vincent & the Grenadines. For six months she continued to trade in northern Europe until 30 July when she left IJmuiden for San Juan (Puerto Rico) and subsequent trade in the Caribbean. In April 2004 she was sold and renamed **Afrodite S**, this sale seeing her commence trade in the Mediterranean and Black Sea. She became **Santa Maria** in 2008 and finally **Santa Maria I** in 2011. As such she was recycled at Aliaga in April 2012. She was photographed outward bound from Eastham in 1975. Falkenbergs Varv was established in 1946 and remains in business for ship repairs and occasional construction of new vessels.

(David Gallichan)

From Sweden, we move to Finland. During the 1970s, a large number of ships were built in Finnish shipyards for the Russian state merchant fleet. Like so many aspects of the regimented Russian regime, the various classes of ship were given a project number and eleven ships of Project 613 were built at the Laivateollisuus yard in Turku between 1978 and 1980. They were named from **Baltiyskiy-101** to **Baltiyskiy-111** although **Baltiyskiy-104** was renamed **Vasiliy Malov** after only two years in service. Here we see **Baltiyskiy-103** outward bound in the River Elbe on 14 August 2007. She was launched on 22 February 1978 and completed on 17 October. Renamed **Aressa** in 2009, the **Baltiyskiy-103** has remained in Russian ownership throughout her career. The Laivateollisuus shipyard was established in 1945. Valmet bought the yard in 1973 although it traded as an independent subsidiary until Laivateollisuus Valmet Oy was formed in 1983. Three years later it merged with Wärtsilä and the Laivateollisuus yard was demolished in 1988. A local street name reminds residents of the yard's existence.

(Dominic McCall)

Uudenkaupungin Työvene Oy (now known in English as Uki Workboat Oy) is located at Uusikaupunki on the west coast of Finland. Although the population is Finnish-speaking, the town's Swedish name (Nystad) is also commonly used and the shipyard is known in Swedish as Nystads Varv. Completed at the yard in March 1975 was the refrigerated vessel **Lindo**. Her owner was Captain Gustaf Erikson whose company had been established in 1913 and which was renowned for its sailing vessels. Its first steamship was bought in 1937 and a decade later it bought its first newbuilding. The **Lindo** was one of 25 new vessels bought by the company since then. She remained under Erikson control after being renamed **Igloo Lion** in 1986. Sold and renamed **Sunny Lisa** in 1995 she retained that name after purchase by Russian owners in 2005. We see her at IJmuiden on 29 June 2008.

(Kevin Jones)

We now look at coasters built in Norway, beginning in the south-east of the country and moving clockwise around the coast. In 1978 six identical coasters were delivered to Bergen-based KS AS Coaster. The first and last ones came from the same yard, the other four were built at four different yards. Initially of 299grt, they certainly added a new profile to coasters of this paragraph. They were multipurpose pallet carriers with a capacity for 22 lorries which gained access via a stern ramp and they had a 32TEU container capacity. The most obvious feature, however, was the large foremast and 28-tonne derrick. All six vessels soon began to visit Goole and we see **Coaster Betty** outward bound from that port on 3 June 1978. She was built by Lindstøl Skips & Båtbyggeri at Risør and, like her five sisterships, she was lengthened by 13 metres by Georg Eides Sønner at Høylandsbygd and this increased her gross tonnage to 475grt. In April 1980 all six vessels were taken back by the main crediitor and re-sold. The **Coaster Betty** became **Coast Narvik** in February 1981 and later sales saw her renamed **Folgefonn** in 1985 and **Firda** in 1993. By 2007 her distinctive mast and derrick had been removed.

(Laurie Schofield)

The **Jylland**, outward bound in Swansea Bay on 24 January 1976, was completed at the Lindstøl yard in October 1973 and has a much more conventional appearance than that of the **Coaster Betty**. With an initial overall length of just under 50 metres, she was lengthened by 14 metres in 1980. In 1989 she was sold within Norway and renamed **Steinbjørn**. She left northern Europe in mid-April 2002 following sale to owners in Alexandria and, then renamed **Nader I** under the flag of Tonga, she began to trade mainly in the eastern Mediterranean. A further sale in 2006 saw her become **Bassma-S** and she arrived at Aliaga for recycling in early May 2010. The Lindstøl shipyard continues to build vessels but these now range from crew boats to mega yachts.

(Nigel Jones)

The brief outline of the shipyards mentioned in this book indicates that European shipbuilding has not fared well since the 1970s. One notable exception is the Båtservice shipyard at Mandal. Opened in 1948, it has gone from strength to strength and remains active in many areas of engineering. This vessel was completed in October 1970 as *Freja Buur* for Danish owners. On her maiden voyage she took a cargo of fertiliser from Porsgrunn to Randers and after arrival was open to all the investors, many of whom were members of the Rotary Club in Randers. She was then taken on a long-term charter delivering potatoes to Southampton from the French port of Tréguier. In September 1973 she was bought by Norwegian owners and renamed *Stenberg*, becoming *Frakt* following a sale three years later and then *Anders Bas* in January 1984 after another sale within Norway. In April 1984 she was rebuilt as a self-discharger and fitted with a Caterpillar excavator. We see her passing Skudenesfjord on 6 May 2002. She was still in service in 2016.

(Tony Hogwood)

The **Smedesund**, photographed at Oslo on 23 August 1979, was launched at the shipyard of Brødrene Lothe in Haugesund on 24 November 1973 and completed on 11 January 1974. Sold within Norway in 1981, she was renamed **Kvitsøy** and was acquired by Lebanese interests in early 1994 and was renamed **Britta K** on 2 February. She was then converted to a livestock carrier at Emden and departed for Alexandria and the Middle East via IJmuiden on 2 April 1994. She has remained in service since that time. Brødrene Lothe was established in 1946 but its first vessel was not launched until a decade later. The yard closed in 1984.

(the late John Wiltshire)

The **Arabian Reefer** is seen at Dubai on 15 February 2000. This refrigerated vessel was completed in March 1972 at the yard of Georg Eides Sønner in Høylandsbygd. After just two years in the ownership of Bergen-based Alf Utkilen, she was sold to owners in Reykjavik and renamed **Ljosaberg**. She became **Isberg** in 1990 and then **Ljosafoss** in 1991. She left northern Europe in June 1992 after purchase by owners in Bahrain, being renamed **Badr**. Subsequent changes of name saw her become **Gulf River** (1995), **Arabian Reefer** (1998), **Sara** (2005) and finally **Al Yamama** (2006). Under this name she was delivered for recycling at Gadani Beach in April 2011. The shipyard was established in 1955 by brothers Johannes and Gerhard Eide in honour of their father, also a shipbuilder. Financial problems in the late 1970s resulted in eventual bankruptcy in 1983. Two subsidiaries survived and combined as Eide Marine Sevices in 1992. This has become hugely successful and, with head office still in Høylandsbygd, now has subsidiary companies in China, Brazil and the Netherlands.

(Roger Hurcombe)

This vessel was a product of Fiskerstrand Verft and she began life as a typical shelterdecker of 297grt. She was ordered by AS Frendo but was sold during construction and was completed as **Ull Gard** for Frigg Shipping & Co in May 1973. Four years later, a sale to Oslo-based owners saw her become **Leca Bulk** and in June 1980 she was bought by Sinus Bulk Shipping, of Sandnes, and renamed **Gravel Bulk**. She was soon converted to a self-discharger as seen here when outward bound in the River Ouse. A sale in September 1991 saw her become **Ingrid Maria** and she continued to work as a self-discharger. The next sale saw her become **Fosenbulk** in 1997 and eight years later she was acquired by owners in Chile and renamed **Amatista**. A further conversion saw her fitted with two deck cranes in order to work along the coast of Chile distributing feed to fish farms.

(David Gallichan)

The **Vesturland** was delivered as **Hvalsnes** from Fiskerstrand Verft in November 1973. She was renamed **Frendo Hvalsnes** in 1974 but reverted to her original name in the following year and then became **Vesturland** for Icelandic owners in 1976. We see her in the River Ouse on 7 June 1979. Her final change of name came in 1982 when she was renamed **Valur**. A decade later, on 22 October 1992, she stranded at Vyborg and was subsequently broken up. The Fiskerstrand shipyard was established in 1909 by Peder E Fiskerstrand and continues to be busy with repairs, conversions and the building of ferries and supply ships.

(Laurie Schofield)

In 1972 Frendo had ordered a coaster from Brattvåg Skipsinnredning but this contract was taken over in 1973 by James Tyrrell Ltd, of Arklow. She was launched on 12 December 1973 and delivered as **Murell** in January of the following year. In 1988 she was sold to a company associated with James Fisher & Sons plc, of Barrow, and having been bareboat chartered to Dennison Shipping, of Kirkwall, was renamed **Hoxa Sound**. After this company collapsed in 1994, the ship was taken back and later renamed **Teal I**. In 1997 she was bought by Alderney Shipping and became **Ortac** and we see her leaving Southampton for Plymouth on 27 May 1997 soon after

purchase. She left northern Europe in 2001 and transferred to the flag of Panama as **Margot**. She left Mounts Bay in late December and was reported at St Vincent in the Cape Verde Islands on 14 January 2002. She was renamed **MCV Express** in 2005 by which time she was trading mainly between Miami and Haiti. In 2012 she was reported by some sources to have been renamed **Oma** but her fate is unknown. Brattvåg Skipsinnredning was established in the 1940s and is now known as VARD AS, a company with yards throughout the world and whose main shareholder is Fincantieri.

(Chris Bancroft)

One of the oldest and longest lasting shipyards in Norway is that of Salthammer Båtbyggeri in Vestnes. It was established by L H Salthammer in 1896 and remains in business building ferries, large workboats and also fabricates and assembles heavy steel structures and components for other customers. Launched at the yard on 16 April 1971 was the **Norimo**. The ship was completed for Norwegian owners at the Aukra Bruk shipyard. Sold to Dutch owners and renamed **Munte** in 1974, she entered the fleet of Oost Atlantic Lijn and was renamed **Atlantic River** in 1981. She was photographed in the River Elbe on 26 June 1995. In mid-December 2001, she suffered serious engine problems when on passage from Dundalk to Rotterdam and had to be towed to her destination for repairs. In fact she was laid up at Ridderkerk and was renamed **Antic River** in late June 2002. She never traded as such but sold again, she left Ridderkerk on 15 May 2003 as **City of Dublin**, heading for Livorno via Vigo. By the end of 2003 she was trading between Pondicherry in India and Colombo in Sri Lanka. In mid-December 2009 she arrived at Jamnagar in India for recycling.

(Author's collection)

The **Patricia** was launched at the Aukra Bruk shipyard in Aukra on 15 October 1971 and delivered as **Südfjord** on 27 November to German operator Bauer & Hauschildt. She was lengthened by 12 metres in 1978. A decade later she was bought by Irish owners, mainly to transport stone from quarries in the south of Ireland. We see her leaving Swansea on 5 August 1990 at the start of a voyage to Wicklow. The year 1994 saw a sale to Mexican owners who abbreviated her name to **Pat**. She was detained at Santo Domingo in late December 1996 because of her owners' debts. On 22 September 1998 she was reported to have run aground in the Isabela River in Santo Domingo as a result of Hurricane Georges and she was then abandoned. The Aukra Bruk shipyard was estabished in 1949 and has built ships of all kinds since that time. It remains in business and is now part of the Fincantieri group.

(Nigel Jones)

Another vessel from the Aukra Bruk yard, the **Estetal** was launched on 7 August 1972 and completed on 18 November for Hamburg-based Julius Hauschildt. In 1984 the ship was badly damaged by fire and was bought by Svendborg Skibsværft. She was towed to Svendborg to be rebuilt as a livestock carrier. Upon completion, ownership changed in bewildering manner during the mid-1980s as companies failed, merged or simply changed name. The ship herself was renamed **Amelia** in 1985. In 2004, she was sold to Vroon, of Breskens, a major competitor of her Danish owners, and she was renamed **Galloway Express** on 24 September. Having changed ownership, the ship had to meet certain Australian rules for the transport of livestock. Older ships found it impossible to meet the rules although, oddly, she would have been acceptable had she remained in Danish ownership. It was decided immediately that she would have to be recycled and only three days after being renamed she left Singapore for the breakers' yard in Chittagong.

(Bernard McCall)

The **Nor Viking** was launched at the Sterkoder shipyard in Kristiansund in May 1977 and delivered to Swedish owners four months later as **Norrviken**. She was one of four vessels delivered to Sweden between January 1977 and January 1978. In late 1988 she was acquired by the Wilson Group and renamed **Norro** under the Norwegian flag. She became **Nor Viking** four years later following a sale within Norway and was photographed near Haugesund on 25 May 2006. She continues to trade in 2016. The Sterkoder shipyard opened on 23 August 1916 and became part of the UMOE Group as Umoe Sterkoder on 7 February 1991. The yard then concentrated on the construction of large trawlers and supply ships but it struggled throughout the 1990s and was faced with closure in 1999 after five consecutive years of heavy losses. Eventual closure as a shipbuilding yard was inevitable but the Kristiansund site remains open as a base for heavy engineering.

(Bernard McCall)

From its foundation in 1884 until the 1960s, Ørens Mek Veksted shipyard in Trondheim built mainly passenger boats, tugs and fishing vessels. Then it started to build coasters and in the 1970s constructed many of a standard 299grt design for Bergen-based Paal Wilson. One of these was **Finno**, launched on 31 August 1970 and delivered on 2 November. Like many of her sisterships, she was lengthened with a 15 metre section being added in October 1977. We see her in the River Trent outward from Gunness on 7 June 1995. She passed through the hands of several Wilson subsidiary companies and was eventually laid up at Slikkerveer in February 2001. Later in the year she was sold to Panamanian flag operators and left Rotterdam for the Caribbean via La Coruña on 24 November. She was renamed **Perla I** in early December. In late October 2003 she was sold and renamed **Aljusi** but remained in the Caribbean, trading mainly between Port of Spain and Puerto Cabello. She disappeared from movement reports in 2005 but is understood to be still in service. The Ørens shipyard closed in 1987.

(John Mattison)

The **Baltic Trader** approaches Trondheim on 10 June 2007. She is a typical coaster in a country where much domestic general cargo is still carried by sea. This fact, coupled with a lack of infrastructure in many small ports, explains the continued and widespread use of the pallet carrier concept. All that is needed for handling cargo is a short length of quay - the ship with its cranes, sideports and cargo elevators will do the rest. The ship was launched by Orens Mek Verksted on 31 December 1974 and delivered to Lys-Line as **Lysfoss** on 25 May 1975. In 1982 she was acquired by J P Strøm which traded as Stream Line and changed the ship's name to **Tinto**. Five years later, she was extensively modified for pallet handling. She was lengthened by 15 metres, her two 3.5 tonne derricks were replaced by a 25 tonne crane, a new 10-tonne derrick was fitted to her foremast, and two cargo elevators were placed behind the new sideport on the starboard side. She became **Baltic Trader** following sale in 2002. Since 2012 she has been owned in South Africa and serves the remote island of Tristan da Cunha from Cape Town, her name being most unsuitable for that trade.

(Uwe Jakob)

The **Toste Jarl**, outward bound from Goole on 24 February 1979, was launched on 23 July 1970 at the Vaagen Verft yard in Kyrksæterøra and was delivered in October 1970 to Det Nordenfjeldske D/S-selskab, of Trondheim. In 1965 this shipyard took over from Grøtvaagen Verft which had opened in 1919 and the yard closed in 1987. The **Toste Jarl** proved to be the only coastal cargo ship built at the yard during the decade although coastal tankers and roll-on/roll-off vessels were constructed there. Although she did not appear in movement reports, she was a regular visitor to Humber ports. After a decade in service the **Toste Jarl** was sold and renamed **Betty-K-V**. It may be assumed that she then traded in the Caribbean. Later changes of name saw her become **Andre-Paul** (1995), **Atlantis Mariner I** (1999), **Laila** (2006), **Laila I** (2007) and finally **Ocean Blue** (2010). She sank on 22 September 2010 when 80 nautical miles south of the Dominican Republic whilst on passage from Haina to Puerto Cabello, Venezuela, with a cargo of cardboard. Her crew of seven was rescued by the Liberian-flagged container ship **Adrian**.

(Laurie Schofield)

Our only featured shipyard in the Faroe Islands is Skala Skipasmidja at Skala. Jørgen Steenberg's Steencoasters company co-operated with this yard and ordered four new ships from the yard, the third one being launched as **Hanne Steen** but delivered in December 1972 to Steencoasters as **Helle Steen**. In November 1977 she was sold to J Lauritzen and renamed **Hellelil**. She was badly damaged by a fire in the accommodation when berthed at Mostyn on 13 January 1980 and was towed away to Århus four months later. Sold in September 1980 she was renamed **Dana**, this being changed to **Dana Guro** after a sale to Norwegian owners in late November 1981. She became **Friborg** following a sale within Norway in August 1994. She was photographed at Dunball Wharf on 18 November 2005 after arrival from Leixoes. In the following month she was sold to a Dutch broker and arrived at 's Gravendeel to lay up. In October 2008 she was bought by owners in Tema, Ghana, and left Rotterdam on 27 October. She was renamed **Jojo** in 2009 and was broken up in Ghana in May 2013. Skala Skipasmidja opened in 1901 and was taken over by Tórshavnar Skipasmidja in 1997. An investment company took over in 2004 and four years later changed the name to MEST, the letters representing the four areas of current work: Machine, Electricity, Steel and Timber.

(Cedric Catt)

Our journey through Europe now takes us eastwards to Poland. The *Haslo* was launched at the Gdanska Lenina Shipyard on 28 January 1976 and was delivered to Norwegian owners as *Ask* on 31 March. She remained in Norwegian ownership following a sale in 1982 when she became *Beito* and then five years later she joined the Paal Wilson fleet as *Haslo*. On 12 October 2003 she grounded outside Egersund. After refloating with assistance, she was moored at Egersund for inspection and remained there until 18 November when she departed for Klaipeda after sale. Renamed *Mariam* this was changed to *Altrans* in mid-May of the following year. A sale in 2010 saw her become *Sarp K* and she arrived at Aliaga for recycling in early April 2012. We see her as *Haslo* at County Wharf, Falmouth, on 1 April 1997 after arrival from Porsgrunn.

(Bernard McCall)

This ship was launched as *Soknatun* at the Gdanska Lenina shipyard on 9 August 1972 and delivered in November to Norwegian owner O H Meling, of Stavanger. This shipyard was established in 1945 on the site of two former German shipyards that had been badly damaged during the Second World War. It became famous in 1980 as the birthplace of Solidarnosc, the first non-Communist trade union in the Soviet bloc. The yard continues to build ships. After various sales within Norway, *Soknatun* became *Bulk Master* in 1993 and then *Loyal Trader* two years later. She was photographed at Medina Wharf, Cowes, on 25 May 1999 after making the short voyage from Southampton. She sailed to Dublin on the following day. She became *Lona* after sale to Swedish owners in 2002 and since 2013 has been laid up at Hälle in Norway.

(Brian Ralfs)

The Wisla shipyard is located on the River Vistula in Gdansk. The yard can trace its history back to 1889 when a facility was constructed for repairing icebreakers. Although mainly a repair yard throughout its history, it has also undertaken construction and remains in business building fishing vessels, modules and sections of larger ships. The **Barlinek** was the last of three coasters constructed in the early 1970s, the design being given the name B457. She arrived at Szczecin on 5 April 1986 and during a ten-week stay her masts and two 3-tonne derricks were removed. In 1992 she was sold to owners in Nigeria and was renamed **Princess Deborah**. She left Szczecin on 14 April 1992, heading for Venice but by the end of the year she was trading between Apapa/Lagos and Tema. A sale within Nigeria saw her become **Suwe Star** in 2001 but nothing further is known about her after she was reported at Abidjan on 30 June 2001. She is still listed in registers. She was photographed in the River Ouse on 24 May 1979.

(Laurie Schofield)

The town of Tczew is located on the Vistula River about 22 miles (35km) south-east of Gdansk. From 1888 it possessed a workshop for repairing river vessels. This steadily grew in size and on 28 March 1954 Tczewska Stocznia Rzeczna (Tczewska River Shipyard) was legally established. There followed rapid expansion but the collapse of the communist regime in Poland resulted in financial problems from 1991. The yard was eventually declared bankrupt in 2004 but amazingly production continued although at a much lower rate. The company was eventually liquidated on 21 January 2011. The **Sea Maas**, the second of two sisterships, was launched on 31 August 1973 and delivered to Freight Express-Seacon in January 1974. In 1986 she was renamed **Glencloy** after sale to Glenlight Shipping and she was fitted with a deck crane. Sold and renamed **Benfield** in 1994, she later became **Victoria IV** (1999), **Kristina** (2005) and **FM Express** (2010). She was destroyed by fire off the coast of Colombia on 10 March 2013, her crew of 8 having been rescued. Again she is seen outward bound in the River Ouse.

(David Gallichan)

The **Sophia-V**, seen in the River Ouse on 23 March 1979, was the last of six sister vessels built by Wroclawska Stocznia Rzeczna (Wroclaw River Shipyard) in the heart of Poland. The first two in the series were built for the Frendo group. In the 1980s all six ships in the series were sold and the **Sophia-V** became **Bulk Wave** in 1981. In May 1982 she was sold to Panamanian-flag operators and on 28 May 1982 she left Rotterdam at the start of a voyage to Miami. After just over one year trading along the coast of the USA, she returned to Rotterdam on 2 July 1983 and was laid up. In mid-1984 she returned to trade in northern Europe as **Bulk Wave**. Sold and renamed **Saez** in 1986, she became **Andorinha** in late 1989 after sale to Portuguese interests. She left Vlissingen for Luanda on 12 January 1990 and commenced trade in Angola. She is reported to have been sold to Nigerian owners in 1994, being renamed **Blessed Mama**, but nothing has been heard about her since 1996. One of the sisterships was also sold to Nigeria.

(Laurie Schofield)

The **Tarnica** is another product of Wroclawska Stocznia Rzeczna and she dates from 1970. She is something of a mystery vessel. One source suggests that she was deleted from registers in 1987 but this is clearly incorrect as this photograph was taken at Gdansk on 6 August 2003. Then owned in Poland and registered at Szczecin, she was classified as an oil/sludge tanker having eight tanks and fitted with heating coils. Since that time, she has been acquired by Russian owners and is now classified as a waste disposal vessel. She is usually based at Kaliningrad and is still named **Tarnica**. The shipyard was on the River Odra and was 350 kilometres from the sea. Used mainly for the construction of inland vessels, the yard was established in 1928 and closed in 1996. Part of the area is now used by the Odratrans Shipyard. In the 1930s, parts for German submarines were fabricated at the yard which was occupied by the Russian army in 1945/46.

(Dominic McCall)

From northern Europe we move south and initially look at some ships built in Spanish shipyards. We start on the northern coast, not far from the French border, and move westwards. It was in the 1930s that Victorio Luzuriaga, having built a smelter in Pasajes, began to repair and later build fishing vessels. The shipyard of Astilleros Luzuriaga was opened in October 1943. This coaster was launched at the Luzuriaga yard on 16 February 1976 and completed as *Eslava* in June of that year for Bilbao-based Luis de Otero. The ship was sold within Spain in 1991 but the new owners soon faced financial difficulties and the ship was laid up at Bilbao from 12 September 1992. Sold to Syrian owners by the Banco Credíto Internacional, she left Bilbao on 23 August 1993 with Tartous as her destination. Now named *Al Khalil III* she was converted to a livestock carrier. Renamed *Al Mahmoud III* in 1997 and *Asalah III* in 2004, she was recycled at Suez in 2009.

(David Gallichan)

The *Punta Izkiro* was launched by Astilleros Luzuriaga on 17 March 1978 and delivered in December of that year to Naviera Jaizkibel. We see her passing Penarth Head when outward bound from Cardiff on 22 April 1987. In early 1988 she was sold within Spain and renamed *Neila*. As such she arrived at Vlissingen in tow in December 1989 and was later towed to Moerdijk where she remained for most of 1990. Towards the end of that year she was sold to Cypriot-flag operators and renamed *Leila*. On 6 April 1992, she left Antwerp, heading initially for Madras and then on to Singapore where she arrived on 31 May. She had been sold and was renamed *Ummeedah* under the Maldives flag. She became *Ocean Express* in 2009 and was recycled at Aliaga in late 2010. The yard had mixed fortunes and was sold and renamed in 1995.

(Bernard McCall)

The Astilleros Balenciaga shipyard is located at Zumaya near the mouth of the River Urola between San Sebastian and Bilbao. It was founded in 1921 and continues to build ships of all kinds including fishing vessels, tugs, supply ships and ferries. The **Sota Aranzazu** was launched at the yard on 24 April 1978 and completed on 6 November. In 1991 she was sold and renamed **Binissalem** to work on the Trans-Balear service linking Valencia to Palma and we see her on 19 July 1997. After ten years serving this route she was sold to Greek owners and she was fitted with a deck crane. Now named **Evia**, this was modified to **Eyboia** in 2004 and later in the year she became **Georgios S**. She remained in Greek ownership following a sale in 2005 when she became **Elwood**.

(Author's collection)

She arrived at Greenore on 3 December 2005 and was detained following a port state control inspection. Twelve days later she departed for Dublin because her berth at Greenore was required for another ship but on 5 February 2006 she was towed from Dublin to Rotterdam by the tug **Thor Goliath**. In 2006 a further sale saw her renamed **Cote Aranzazu** and we see her laid up at the Dockside shipyard in IJsselmonde on 16 April 2007. In mid-2008 she was understood to have been sold and a crew of five Ghanians manned the ship. A year later they returned home after a claim of non-payment of wages. She was eventually sold for recycling and was towed from Rotterdam to Harlingen and then via the Prinses Margriet Canal to Kootstertille for breaking up. Her upperworks had to be removed prior to the voyage so that she could pass beneath bridges.

(Koos Goudriaan)

Photographed at Wisbech on 29 September 1999, the **Eiffel Star** was built by Astilleros y Talleres de Celaya SA at Erandío on the River Nervion near Bilbao. She was launched on 1 June 1977 and delivered as **Extramar Oeste** in December to Naviera Extramar SA, Bilbao. She was sold out of the Spanish fleet in 1994 and was renamed **Eiffel Star**. She left Europe in 2002 after being sold to Marítima del Plata, of Montevideo, and was renamed **Nobleza** under the flag of Uruguay. She then commenced trade between that country and Argentina. In 2013 she was sold to owners in Argentina and, after removal of her main engine, was delivered for service as a river barge. The shipyard was established in 1928 and became Astilleros y Talleres de Celaya in 1965 following reorganisation of the Spanish shipbuilding industry. In the 1970s, the yard built several impressive sail training ships for countries in South America but was forced to close in 1983.

(John Robinson)

This ship was built by Astilleros del Cadagua at Bilbao, Cadagua being the name of a river in Bilbao. The yard was founded by W Emilio González in 1944 and was merged with two other yards in 1985. She was launched at the yard on 27 May 1975 and completed as *Fer Balear* on 10 January 1976. She was sold in 1985 and was renamed *Miami Super* for trade between Miami and Port au Prince. She returned to Europe in 1988 and traded initially along the Portuguese coast and then more widely as *Luso Vouga* for Lisbon-based Lusonautis. In late summer 1990 she returned to Spanish ownership as

Cabo S. Vicente. Following purchase by Greek owners in 1994 she was renamed *Evita* and her trading area became the eastern Mediterranean and Black Sea. She was renamed *Apollon* in 1999 and *Altsi* in 2001. We see her thus named in Piraeus Roads on 5 September 2004. Later changes of name saw her become *Juliana* (2005), *Terek al Saad* (2008), *Baraket Alraman* (2010) and finally *Sea Karam* (2013). She arrived for recycling at Aliaga in late August 2014.

(David Oldham)

This coaster was launched at the Basse-Sambre-Corcho shipyard in Santander on 30 October 1970 and delivered as **Malladas** to Spanish owners based in Gijon on 1 April 1971. She was rebuilt as a container ship with fixed guides in 1977. In 1980 she was sold and entered the fleet of Thomas Watson (Rochester) Ltd as **Lady Rhoda**. On 23 June 1989 she sank approximately ten miles off Vigo following a collision with a Moroccan fishing vessel. Sadly her crew of six did not survive and only the body of her master was recovered.

This image dates from 1984 and shows her about to pass beneath the Humber Bridge. Shipbuilding in that area of Santander can be dated back to 1878 but it has certainly not been a story of success. Mergers and restructuring have been a constant necessity and Basse-Sambre-Corcho was established in 1961, thanks to funding from Belgium. This was one of the last ships to be built by the yard which was taken over by Chantiers de l'Atlantique in 1971. Losses continued and the yard finally closed in 1988.

(David Gallichan)

The rowers relax as **Vega de Danubio** passes Penarth beach outward bound to Bilbao with a cargo of scrap on 15 June 1984. The coaster was launched at the yard of Maritima del Musel in Gijón on 12 May 1976 and she was delivered in August of that year. She was the first of a pair of ships ordered from this yard by Naviera Continental, based in Bilbao. Both were sold out of the Spanish fleet in 1991 and the **Vega de Danubio** was renamed **Danube** at Pasajes while undergoing repairs between 15 October and 29 November 1991. She was renamed **Mirri** at Rotterdam in mid-June 1992. On 2 February 1993 she left Grangemouth and sailed via Gibraltar and Suez to Shanghai. In 1998 she was renamed **Wan Sheng** by Chinese owners and then **Jin Hai Ou** in 2001. The Maritima del Musel shipyard was established in 1943. It was the victim of much unrest in the late 1970s and in 1983 it was forced to merge with two other private shipyards in the city to form Naval Gijón. This company struggled on for 25 years but eventually succumbed in 2008.

(Bernard McCall)

The Duro Felguera shipyard in the Spanish port of Gijón was part of a huge enterprise that was begun by Pedro Duro Benito in 1858. Initially the company was involved in coal mining and iron and steel production. From the early 1960s, the company began to specialise in manufacture rather than raw materials. The yard was another of the three that merged to form Naval Gijón in 1983. The **Algalo** was launched on 6 April 1977 and delivered to Naviera García Miñaur on 25 June. We see her outward bound in the River Ouse on 24 April 1979. In late 1988 she was sold, renamed **Noble Horse**, and was immediately laid up at Santander. Presumably the sale was never completed

and the ship returned to service as **Algalo** in October 1989. In mid-1990 she was certainly sold and began to trade in central America until late 1992. She left Houston for Garston on 21 December and after a two week stay at the Mersey port departed on 30 January 1993, heading for Singapore where she arrived on 17 March. She was then renamed **Shan Master** and began trading between Hong Kong and Shantou in China. Later changes of name saw her become **Soonwan** (1994), **Dona Amparo** (2003) and **Hanako** (2005). She continues to trade as such in the Far East under the flag of the Philippines.

(Laurie Schofield)

This vessel was built by Astilleros y Construcciones Meira, near Vigo, and was launched on 30 May 1972. She was delivered to Danish owner Jørgen Steenberg as *Birte Steen* on 31 March 1973. An order for a sister vessel was cancelled because of problems with the Spanish ship finance scheme. In November 1974 she was sold for a huge price to a British leasing company for operation by Stephenson Clarke and was renamed *Brightling*. She was photographed in the River Mersey at Eastham. A sale in 1980 saw her renamed *Mor Star* for trade in the southern USA and Caribbean. She became *Caribic Star* in 1986 and then in May 1987 she was purchased by a Danish leasing company and renamed *Kirsten Lea*. The first few months of 1989 saw

her sail from Colombia to Houston then via Suez to Eilat with eventual arrival in Bangkok in mid-May. Now renamed *Sang Thai Fortune*, she became *Kang Song 3* in 1999 and finally *Kang Song* in 2003. She was broken up at Jingjiang in China during June 2014. The building yard, generally known as Ascón, was established in 1969 by the merger of two other shipyards and had a stormy existence. It was taken over by Astilleros del Atlántico, based in Santander, in 1977 but a series of disastrous orders led to financial problems and the Spanish government ordered the yard's closure in 1984, a decree which led to much social unrest and bitterness.

(David Gallichan)

From Spain, we move to Italy. We could devote at least two pages to the history of this vessel. She was launched at the Visentini shipyard at Porto Viro on 1 August 1975, one of only three coasters built at the yard during the 1970s, and was completed as **Centotre** for the builder's own account in June 1976. She became **Depatre** in 1988, **Blue Dream** in 1991 and **Nancy** in 1994. We see her thus named when outward bound from 36 Berth Southampton to Lisbon on 8 June 2000. She was sold and renamed **Aliza** in 2002 and then **Beton Leader** in 2004. A small fortune has been spent on her to convert her to a self-sufficient concrete batching ship. Despite the expense, she has been detained at Antwerp for almost two years and then laid up at that port (and elsewhere) for long periods. Established in 1964, the family-owned Visentini yard remains extremely busy building mainly ferries and ro/ro vessels.

(Chris Bancroft)

This vessel was built by one of the most famous shipyards in Italy, namely the Orlando shipyard in Livorno (Leghorn). It was established in 1865 by Luigi Orlando and his 3 brothers. In the 20th century, the yard experienced a series of mergers and demergers and was subsumed within the Fincantieri group in 1984. The latter closed the yard in 1995 but it reopened in the following year thanks to the efforts of its 360 former employees. It closed again in 2002 but reopened under new ownership in 2003, now concentrating on the building of luxury yachts. There is a statue of Luigi Orlando by the site of the original yard.

The *Edarte-1*, photographed at Rijeka on 13 October 2009, was launched in October 1970 and delivered as *Sidervega* in June 1971 to Italsider, the huge Italian producer of steel. For 35 years she carried that company's products around the Mediterranean until sold to Albanian owners in early 2006. She was renamed *Edarte-1* and immediately started to trade between Durres and Split but by 2009 she was trading more widely. She was recycled at Aliaga in September 2010.

(Dominic McCall)

Båtservice Verft, of Mandal (see page 52), established a new building yard at Vindholmen, near Arendal, in the early 1970s. This yard designed and built a successful series of sixteen coasters of 1599gt. We move to Greece and note that the Argo shipyard at Salamis was granted a licence to build six more ships of the same design in the late 1970s, all for an owner based in Andros. The **Argo Valour** was launched on 20 August 1977 and delivered on 26 January 1978. In 1986 she entered the fleet of Charles Willie (Shipping) Ltd and was renamed **Celtic Challenger**. She is seen arriving at Cardiff from Bilbao on 19 September 1992. In July 1995 she was bought by Norwegian operator Nygård Shipping and renamed **Trader Bulk**. Having been fitted with an excavator and rebuilt with a single hold, she was immediately operated under contract to Norstone AS which shipped aggregate from the Stavanger area to ports throughout Europe. In 1996 she went to the Naval Shipyard in Gdynia to be lengthened by 12 metres. She was bought by owners in Kotor, Montenegro, in August 2005 and was renamed **Zelenika**. Sold again in 2011 she became **Caspian Wave** and arrived at Aliaga for recycling in mid-September 2014.

(Nigel Jones)

Fredrik Odfjell represents the third generation of the Odfjell shipping family, major ship owners in Norway. In September 1968 he acquired a company named Frendo AS which was to be the core of a huge series of contracts for small coastal vessels. By 1974, there were 45 ships on order but a market collapse in 1974 led to huge problems and the Frendo Group was liquidated in 1977. The ships had been ordered from over 20 different shipyards throughout Europe including the United Shipyard at Perama in Greece. Many of the orders were cancelled or transferred before or during construction.

The **Chantenay**, seen at Swansea on 14 October 1975, is an example. Launched at Perama for French owners on 24 October 1974, she was delivered in July 1975. Sold to owners in Morocco in 1984, she was renamed **Sefrou** and became **Ada K** in 1993. She traded mainly in the western Mediterranean but a sale in 1996 saw her renamed **Sophia** and she moved to the eastern Mediterranean and Black Sea. Later renamed **Sophia II** (1999), **Bruno** (2003), **Edarte** (2004), **Sea Park** (2006) and **Green Flower** (2007), she was eventually recycled at Aliaga in July 2011.

(the late John Wiltshire)

Readers may be surprised to learn about shipyards in central Europe and we now turn to a selection of those. Belgrade is now the capital of and largest city in Serbia. Formerly in Yugoslavia, it is situated at the confluence of the Danube and Sava rivers. One of its shipyards was named after President Tito who was much admired and whose brand of communism was not to Russia's liking. The shipyard named after him built mainly barges for Danube trading but in 1972 it constructed two low air draught coasters. The second of these was named *Auberg*. Launched on 17 January 1972, she was delivered in March of that year. She was one of the first vessels to be fitted with a hydraulically-operated wheelhouse, in her case moving up and down on a scissor lift. She was photographed when approaching Goole on 29 November 1983. On 31 January 1986, she suffered a fire in her engine room and later sank when about 120 miles south-west of La Rochelle during a passage from Helsingborg to Santander. The building yard is now known as Beograd Brodogradiliste.

(David Gallichan)

On 1 November 1890, Otto Alfred Müller, then aged 31, established a company to import coal from the UK to Germany. Indeed he secured the sole rights to import "Bolsover coal". In 1909 he decided that his requirements would be best served by owning his own fleet. In the late 1960s the company took the unusual step of ordering two vessels from the Angyalfold shipyard in Budapest. Such an order was attractive because of the low price being offered by the builder. The first was launched in 1969 and two further pairs of identical vessels were soon ordered. The **Dolomit**, launched on 10 November 1972, was the last of the six and she was delivered on 18 July 1973. All of them,

named after minerals, were delivered down the Danube to Braila where the superstructure was fitted. In November 1975, she was lengthened by six metres by Motorenwerken in Bremerhaven. Sold out of the Müller fleet in 1983, she was renamed **Orchid Star** and then **Lady Dorothy** in 1984 when acquired by Thomas Watson. Sold a decade later, she was renamed **Dana** and we see her leaving Southampton at the start of a voyage to Pasajes on 11 May 1998. She became **Kris** in 2000 and was wrecked on 27 September 2008 when on passage from Iskenderun to Greece with a cargo of steel.

(Chris Bancroft)

One of the minor problems in arranging a book country-by-country is that political changes move boundaries and alter the names of some countries. Thus the yard that constructed the **Volgo-Balt 215** was in Czechoslovakia when the ship was built in 1978 but is now in Slovakia. Opened in 1898 at Komárno on the River Danube in order to repair river barges, it later started to build such vessels and from the 1960s built a huge number of vessels for Russia. One of these was the **Volgo-Balt 215**, photographed arriving at the Finnish port of Kaskinen on 30 June 2007. Two years later she was sold and renamed **Bellatrix**. Owned in Turkey since 2014, she continues to trade in the eastern Mediterranean and Black Sea. On 1 January 1993, Czechoslovakia was divided into the Czech Republic and Slovakia. The bombing of bridges on the Danube by NATO forces in 1999 posed huge problems for the yard as vessels were unable to navigate the river and the yard fell into disuse. It was eventually revived and now builds the hulls of ships in addition to steelwork for other uses.

(Bernard McCall)

In 1949, several eastern bloc countries formed the Council for Mutual Economic Assistance (Comecon) with Russia as leader. There was no way that Russian shipyards could keep pace with the country's demand for ships in the late 1960s and early 1970s and so it was inevitable that it would place orders with yards in other Comecon nations. Between 1970 and 1973, the Santierul Naval yard in the Romanian port of Constanta built a class of eleven general cargo ships for Russia and followed these with a further four for its own use in 1974. The ships had three holds and three hatches served by three 5-tonne cranes. The second in the series was named **Sosnovets** and remained in Russian ownership until 1998 when she was bought by Cambodian operators and renamed **Seaway**. We see her thus named in Singapore Roads on 14 June 2000. She later traded mainly between Japan and eastern Russia but was deleted from registers in 2012 as her existence was by then in doubt. The shipyard can be dated back to 1892 but was mainly a repair yard until 1950 when ship building began in earnest. It is now one of the biggest yards in the world.

(David Williams)

The shipyard at Turnu Severin on the banks of the River Danube in Romania dates back to 1852. Traditionally a builder of barges for Danube trade, it saw an increased demand for its products in the early 1960s and was extensively rebuilt in 1965/66. In 1972/73, the yard built four ships for the Romanian merchant fleet (NAVROM), the first of these being the **Bega**, photographed at Penzance on 19 April 1973. The ships had six 5-tonne derricks serving three holds and three hatches. It was in 1972, incidentally, that the original Latin name was added and so the town became Drobeta Turnu Severin. She passed westwards through the Bosphorus on 5 July 1996 and disappeared from movement reports. On 6 December, however, she was renamed **Luck II** after being sold. She later became **Pelaginee** (1997), **Pelagos** (1998), **Athos** (2000) and **Ektor** (2002). She was recycled at Mumbai in November 2003.

(Terry Nelder)

The shipyard initially named Santierul Naval Turnu Severin was established in 1852 by Donaudampfschiffahrtsgesellschaft - Danube Steamship Company (DDSC), an Austrian shipping company. The yard was taken over by the Romanian state in 1893 and then traded as Santierul Naval SEVERNAV. Shipbuilding and repairs continue with the yard trading once again as Severnav Shipyards. In September 1979 the yard delivered the **Toplita** to NAVROM, the Romanian state shipping company. She was one of twelve vessels ordered by the company, with a further four shared between Czechoslovakia and Cuba. She was sold in 1997 and renamed **Nora**, becoming **Peter M** in 1999 and **Ali Bey** in 2007. She arrived at Aliaga for recycling in late May 2012. We see the ship when named **Peter M** and at anchor off Istanbul on 22 October 2002.

(Nigel Jones)

In the years following the Second World War, Russian merchant shipping developed in ways that were very different from those taken by shipping elsewhere in Europe. For various reasons mainly related to the communist ideal, market forces were far less important than the need to expand Russia's growing overseas and inland trade. Successive "Five Year Plans" saw new shipyards being built along with new classes of merchant ships. Many of the latter were mainly for inland navigation and the only class of genuine seagoing coasters was the "Soviet Warrior" class of which the **Yakov Reznichenko** is

an example. A total of twenty were constructed between 1968 and 1971 and she was one of eight built at the Okean shipyard in Nikolayev in Ukraine, a yard previously known for building large factory trawlers and bulk carriers. The ships of this design generally carried timber from Russia to northern Europe and this vessel was heading for Goole when photographed from the Humber Bridge in 1984. She became **Timber Sun** after a sale in 1998 **Tamara** in 2003, and then **Real** in 2008. She continues to trade mainly between Japan and ports in the far east of Russia.

(David Gallichan)

As we note elsewhere, there were many shipyards building vessels for Russia's vast waterway system. Some of these yards were in communist-controlled countries and some were in Russia itself. It would be remiss of us to omit a Russian-built ship. The **Volgo-Don 141** was built at the Oka shipyard in Navashino, the Oka river being a tributary of the Volga. The shipyard was opened in 1907 and continues to be a prolific builder. The **Volgo-Don 141**, seen outward bound from St Petersburg on 5 July 2008, is a member of a large class built solely for inland navigation. After the collapse of the communist system in Russia in 1991, newly-privatised ship owners were desperate to find work for their ships and to earn much needed currency. Consequently, two examples of the class were given permission to leave Russia and sail to the southern coast of Finland. To make them more suitable for seagoing, some examples were shortened in 1994 but the vast majority have remained in as-built condition.

(Simon Smith)

We have a solitary ship from a Turkish shipyard. During the 1970s, these yards built mainly for domestic owners but in years to come they would build extensively for owners worldwide. Çelik Tekne Sanayi is a typical example. The yard opened in the Golden Horn area of Istanbul and moved to Tuzla, south of the city, in 1981. It has become one of the largest and the most efficient privately owned shipyards in Turkey, and specialises in building container ships, trawlers and chemical tankers. Like many other Turkish yards, it built vessels for the Turkish merchant fleet in the 1970s and the **Derya-1** was completed at the yard in June 1974. In 1992 she was sold within Turkey and renamed **Kadioglu-I**. On 29 January 1993 she capsized and sank at Mersin whist being towed after grounding the previous evening. She was eventually refloated on 6 July 1993 and a photograph of her at Tuzla in 1993 shows her to be extensively damaged. However, she was virtually rebuilt and re-entered service as **Karaer III** in 1994. We see her at Valletta on 20 October 2001 and she remains busy in 2016.

(the late Fred Kissack)

As we near the end of the book, we move to the Far East where the rapidly-expanding shipbuilding industry was to account for the demise of many yards in Europe. We begin with a vessel built in Japan for Japanese owners. She was launched at the Higaki Zosen shipyard in Imabari on 17 July 1979 and was delivered to her owners as *Princess Toyo* on 10 September. This building yard was established in 1901 and remains in the ownership of the Higaki family. In terms of tonnage and sales revenue it claims to be the largest shipbuilder in Japan and has eight other integrated shipyards and manufacturing sites in the country. Since delivery of the first steel vessel in 1956, over 2250 ships have been built. The *Princess Toyo* became *Ben Thanh* in 1983 and retained this name until 2006 when she was renamed *Tay Do 06* and registered in Saigon. In 2015 she was reported to be trading as *Hai Phuong Sky* and in November 2015 she was noted in the South China Sea and named *Ha Thanh*. We see her as *Ben Thanh* in Singapore Roads on 18 June 2005.

(Nigel Jones)

Seacon was founded as Sea & Continental Waterways Transport Ltd in 1955 and has always prided itself on the 'door-to-door' delivery concept. The appearance of new designs of sea/river ships in the 1970s offered new opportunities to the company and they were keen to acquire some examples. Four sisterships were ordered from Kanrei Zosen in Tokushima, the first of these being the **Sea Humber**. All four were placed under the control of Seacon subsidiary Freight Express-Seacon, established in 1973. She was launched on 4 April 1977 and completed during July. Sold and renamed **Sea Hawk** in 2000, she reverted to **Sea Humber** two years later and is seen heading west along the Kiel Canal in May 2004. She moved to the Mediterranean in 2007 after being sold and renamed **Nildya**. She later became **Warsa** (2008) and **Gabriel** (2009) before arriving at Aliaga for recycling in early July 2011.

(Dominic McCall)

In the early 1970s, plans were made for a huge new steel works (Stålverk 80) in Luleå in northern Sweden along with a rolling mill further south in Gävle. A group of Swedes, realising the transport needs for the new projects, designed a coaster of 1300 tonnes deadweight as being ideal for the Baltic trades and eight ships were ordered from yards in Japan. The ships comprised the Nordship pool and all were given names commencing **Nord**. The third ship to be delivered was the **Nordwest**, completed in February 1977 by Tokushima Sangyo at Komatsushima. Like the other ships, she was largely financed by investors from the island of Gotland. Her master, Carl-Erik Larsson, initially had a 10% share but eventually became sole owner. For over 30 years, he retained command until the ship was sold to Norwegian owners and renamed **Nyfjell** in 2006. With the steel industry in crisis in the 1970s, the Swedish government abandoned Stålverk 80 in 1976 by which time the ships were under construction. Once in service, they had to seek other cargoes. We see the **Nordwest** inward bound at Eastham on 3 September 1977.

(David Gallichan)

A remarkable series of ships was built in eight different Japanese shipyards between 1969 and 1975. The ships were designed by Greek owner George P Livanos in conjunction with the Hakodate Dock Company. They were shallow draught vessels able to navigate far up rivers and 55 examples were built. They were most successful in the southern USA where they were able to sail far up the Mississippi and Missouri rivers to load cargoes for the Caribbean. All had names beginning *Mini L...*. The *Dauria* was delivered from the Yokohama Zosen yard at Chiba as *Mini Lizard* in July 1972 and seems to have spent most of her career under this name in the Mediterranean. In October 1992 she was sold and renamed *Marseille*, becoming *Redo I* a decade later. It was in 2004 that she was renamed *Dauria* and we see her in the Bosphorus on 29 June 2006. She became *Balcar* in 2007 and arrived at Aliaga for recycling in August 2008. Some of the class were gearless, some had two cranes as seen on the *Dauria*, and some had four cranes.

(Martin Penwright)

We now look at another ship built in Japan for local owners. This vessel was built as **Shinryosan Maru** at the Imamura shipyard in Kure. We have no date of launch or delivery; indeed much of the ship's career has been shrouded in mystery. Although we have details of name changes, registers have generally been unable to give information about owners or nationality. We know that her changes of identity saw her become **Sunrise Two** (1987), **Lily Maa** (1990),

Sea Express I (1996), **Obaid** and then **Mona Lisa 1** (1999), **Haydara** (2004), **Al Marwa** (2007) and finally **Sara A** (2010). She was photographed at Sharjah on 11 April 2003, possibly the only time that she has been recorded. When last reported as **Sara A**, she was flying the flag of Sierra Leone and was in Jazeera port in 2011.

(Roger Hurcombe)

With European owners desperate to build up their fleets and many European yards working at full capacity, a small group of German owners negotiated with a Japanese trading house for the construction of seventeen sisterships to be built at seven relatively small yards and this vessel was the first of two built by Rinkai Kogyo at Setoda. She was launched on 9 February 1977 and completed for Fisser & Co as **Sanderskoppel** on 11 April. In 1986 she was acquired by other German owners with management in the hands of an Austrian company and she was renamed **Stefan**. In January 1998 she entered the fleet of the Hull-based Rix Shipping Co Ltd becoming this company's **Lerrix**. She joined two sisterships on what had become the Rix Baltic Line linking Hull to Tallinn, Klaipeda and Riga. We see her heading eastwards along the Kiel Canal on 6 August 2007. Sold in 2010 she was renamed **Leon** but this proved to be shortlived as she arrived at Aliaga for recycling in June of the following year.

(Dominic McCall)

Bell Lines was established in 1936 as George Bell and Company (Dublin) Ltd. It was always a forward-looking company and chartered many coasters for trade around northern Europe. In the mid-1970s, it ordered ten container ships from Kagoshima Dock in Japan. These were delivered between 1976 and 1978. The **Bell Ranger** was launched on 29 September 1976 and completed on 24 December. She was lengthened by 13 metres in 1982. She was unique amongst the ten ships as she was owned in Bremen and chartered to Bell Lines, the other nine all being owned by the company and under the Irish flag.

She was photographed on 22 April 1995 as she approached Avonmouth at the end of a voyage from Waterford. With Bell Lines in financial difficulties in the mid-1990s, she was sold and was briefly renamed **Als** in 1996 before becoming **Perma Glory**. She was renamed **Iran Glory** in 2003 and **Mataf Star** in 2004. Her more recent history is uncertain. Some reports suggest that she was renamed **Moshref** in 2013 and that she transferred from the flag of Iran to that of Panama.

(Bernard McCall)

This vessel was the first of three ordered by Frendo from the Smedvik shipyard at Tjorvåg, south of Ålesund. The hulls were built at the Eid shipyard with completion at the Smedvik yard, the Eid yard being in the Smedvik group. This vessel was launched as **Frendo Danship** in October 1976 but delivered as **Danship** in February 1977. Later in 1977 she was renamed **Atlantic Prosperity** and traded from New York mainly to Miami and Nassau for four years. The year 1982 saw her become **Agate Prosperity** and, with her two sisterships, she was lengthened by 9 metres at Bremerhaven. Later in the year she was sold to Austrian owners and renamed **Mur**. Later sales and changes of name saw her become **Murray** (1991), **Mermaid Sky** (2002) and finally **Asia Hakan** (2007). She was recycled at Aliaga in February 2012. We see her at the Kartal anchorage off Istanbul on 12 August 2009.

(David Dixon)